JUNGLE DANCE

PETRA ABA ASAMOAH

Exemplar Innovations Limited

P.O.BOX 6599 Accra-North, Ghana.

Tel: +233274344000

Email your questions and comments to the author at
info@petraasamoah.com

Cover Design & Layout: Invictüs

ISBN: 978-9988-3-0412-6

Like in choreography, where the movement, sequence and rhythm create one beautiful dance ensemble, so it is in the business world. The need to develop strategic alliances both personal and professional, hard work, tolerance and mutual respect make the dance meaningful. This book shows a classic depiction of how the business world works and teaches how to manoeuvre your way to success.

Jacqueline B-Smith Angmor, A People Enthusiast

Jungle Dance presents an interesting storyline that delves into the romantic, family and corporate life of a strong-willed woman and touches on the evolving culture of women assuming more responsible positions while experiencing, to an extent, the hitherto missing 'masculine' support. This book gives a sneak peak into the world of women emerging to be influential players and their struggle to make the mark.

Grace Sackey, Communications Specialist

Rooted in experience and yet so current - useful for teaching and learning. The intricately woven plot has broad themes of hope, faith, perseverance, integrity, self confidence and humility - life lessons learned the hard way and freely shared for the benefit of men and women of this age.

Abigail Gyimah, Peace, Security and Development Analyst

A candid, impressive and fluent story that draws its readers into an honest account of how its lead characters are able to move rhythmically through the typical adult life. A strongly recommended and inspiring read!

Arthur Mills, Foreign Service Officer

Petra has complete control of her story and her style. The lessons on leadership, corporate management, marriage and integrity are very powerful. Throughout the book, she sprinkles politics, music, history and current affairs, making it relatable to readers of various ages and backgrounds.

Gloria Appoh- Segbawu, Administrator

Taking stock of one's life is critical for success but being able to share that experience helps others navigate the curve faster – therefore contributing to the growth of society. This is a pleasant interface between fiction and non-fiction. Petra shares unreservedly yet imagines boldly.

Henry Nii Dottey APR, Marketing and Communications Specialist.

DEDICATION

To every young person trying to succeed in the world of work:

May you find your place, your voice and your pace.

May your 'dance' be worthy and may the lessons you learn make you a better version of you.

ACKNOWLEDGEMENTS

Special thanks to:

Yusif Agana, Deborah Armah Quaye, Robert Nii Kpakpo Atsem, Aaron Richard Ekow Eshun, Joseph Zotoo, Abigail Gyimah, Victor Tekpetey, Gloria Appoh-Segbawu for asking the questions that triggered the plot of this book.

Abigail Ayensu for being the team lead of the *give-Petra-pressure-until-she-finishes-the-book* squad.

To Yaw Ofosu Larbi, Dr. Denise Mantey and Ebenezer Odumang for reading the manuscript, critiquing it and helping me make it better. I hope you like the final outcome.

To Sena, for everything and for always.

Thank you.

FOREWORD

In Petra's second book, she veers very far off the track of her first book, Sales 101 and ventures into the very exciting realms of modern African fiction. And she delivers a fantastic and intriguing addition to the genre.

Jungle Dance deals with many of the issues and challenges confronting today's African woman that are rarely discussed publicly, but whispered among young African women very furtively and very frequently. What do you do when you are one half of a career power couple and you get a great job offer in another country? Who makes the sacrifice for the other's sacrifice? And when the husband takes a step back for the wife's career, how do the couple manage the judgmental stares and fight back from the extended family?

How does one deal with a toxic work environment and at what point does one put one's physical and emotional well-being ahead of a job? Jungle Dance also deals with issues of emotional intelligence at work, cultural differences and of course a healthy dose of cross country marriages in a very mature and caring manner. The magic of Jungle Dance is that the stories of these amazing women is set within the context of contemporary history and the relationship between Ghana & Nigeria, not just at the political level, but at the corporate, family and personal levels.

Jungle Dance ends with too many untold stories. There's more to the stories of Yomba and Chidi, Bose and Mantse that we cannot wait to hear. It is such a joy and an honour to welcome Petra Aba Asamoah to the esteemed club of phenomenal modern day writers of African fiction. We are waiting eagerly for Jungle Dance II.

Charlotte A. Osei
Lawyer & International Elections Consultant
Accra, Ghana
August 2020

THE JOURNEY TO JUNGLE DANCE

A few days to my thirty-sixth birthday, I began to reflect on the year that was about to end and the very interesting things that had happened to me at work. In 2016, after working for nine years in one company, I had moved on to a new industry, a new environment and a totally new culture. It was a mixed bag of lessons.

On the 15th of March 2019, I asked a few of my friends to help me compile a list of thirty-five questions they would like me to answer relating to my corporate journey. I wanted to write a small book to end my thirty-fifth year and usher in a new year. I felt it was important to document a year that I believe marked a major milestone – my thirty-fifth year. Someone said to me once, "thirty-five is old enough to be wise and young enough to be crazy". I have joked to myself that my default age will always be thirty-five. It is such a nice number. Well, some of my friends got back to me and their questions were indeed, thought-provoking.

As I compiled the questions and reflected on how to answer them, I decided not to write a motivational book as was my original plan or a business-related book like my first book, *Sales 101: What Everyone Should Know About Sales*. Instead, I decided to answer their questions by weaving them into the plot of a fictional book inspired by some of my real-life experiences. The thought of writing fiction was scary and the journey has been one of reflection and self-discovery. Reflection because I have had to go back and replay some of my experiences and truthfully ask myself "could I have done that any differently?" In the same way, I have discovered that our human experience is largely a result of how we react to the situations we encounter rather than what other people do.

This book is a reflection of what I have experienced and observed (closely and from a distance) over close to fifteen years in the corporate world. It reflects my journey – from being a young woman starting out in the corporate world, unsure about herself and my gradual progression into senior management and entrepreneurship.

Even though this is my second book, it is my first foray into the erudite world of literature. I have tried to present the spirit of the times I live in and the historical as well as trending issues as they impact on the characters. It is my hope that the themes of this book will lead to discussions in offices, homes and amongst friends.

Jungle Dance is a euphemism for a myriad of issues, roles, relationships and routes. It is my picture of what the corporate world is – challenging at times, but rewarding also.

Some of the emotions as I have expressed them are raw – reflecting exactly how I felt when these events occurred. I have captured the feelings of despondency, rejection and confusion as I have experienced them and to be authentic, I have also presented the triumphs, the friendships, the joy of having a supportive spouse to lean on and the blessing of being a working mother with all its difficulties.

I hope this book inspires and motivates you. But above all, I hope you enjoy reading it – because reading is entertainment too.

Petra Aba Asamoah
June, 2020

CONTENT

Part One

If you want to change the world, go home and love your family

Mother Teresa

PROLOGUE

Jungle Dance – The Work Life

Many tides – Life
Braced some... overtaken by a few
Counting blessings, considering setbacks too
Roses with thorns

Honey with stings
Self-arranged on pedestals

Or placed there by other mortals?
Politics and pungent sycophancy it is.
The jungle dance – spinning around in circles
Did society claim progress was required?
Did society project that skills will lead to progress?
Society? Was society sure? Wait.

These are monsters! Blood sucking demons – cloaked in suits
of many colours.

Suit and tie... bees that sting with style.
Work life.

Not all men lie, but many lie as their breath
Not all women lie, but many lie as their air
The head of the table – *board* they call it.

Presides over a brood
Broods over a den of thieves and a bandit of liars
In public – projected, praised and hailed
Doors shut? A box like Pandora's... deadly
Work life.

Pomposity, poignant poise with no purpose?
Or passion and pin-point precision
"Life is not a bed of roses," daddy said.
Did I understand it? Not until then.

Then when the work life explained it – so real.
The work life? A jungle dance... spinning and spinning

But dance we must, with style and focus...
Dance we will to glorify the giver.
We will dance.

Corporate? Jungle dance.
Business? Jungle dance.
What is this work life?

A walk, jump, slide or a fall?
The work life — a maze.
We dance… and we win.

Sometimes we lose. But we must enjoy the dance
Because life as we know it, is not a rehearsal.

This is IT.

Work life is life.
Selah

©Petra Aba Asamoah
Accra - April 2019

CHAPTER ONE

She woke up around the same time every night. In the same fashion – uneasy and breaking out in a cold sweat. It was every night, but Sunday nights into Monday were worse. She would wake up in real panic, like one haunted by ghosts. Just that now, it was not the result of binging on too many horror movies. Morning beckoned and in *short* eight hours, she will repeat the weekly routine of questions, *never-ending questions* and the scornful manner in which Bose[1] will ask: "Is that all? Is that all you have to report?"

"Yes, madam, that is all for this week." *And you can shove it up your...* was her other response – but only in her head.

She could never say that out loud. There was too much at stake and there was no denying it: she was suffering from a severe case of 'Bose-phobia', as Chidi called it.

She glanced at her phone to check the time – 00:05. It *was* Monday. She needed to go back to bed. Yet, she was wide

---

[1]Bose is a Yoruba name which is a diminutive of *Abosede*. It is pronounced as 'Bosε'

awake and anxious. This was her *normal*: the inability to sleep throughout the night, the anxiety and the constant feelings of inadequacy. Was it ever going to get better? Was quitting a solution? Or, did she have a medical condition that needed to be attended to? She had initially joked about it, posting a couple of times on her Facebook page: *"Sleep is for the weak"*. There was a 'gang' on Facebook who boasted of their nocturnal prowess and she liked that she could identify with something, at least, to make sense of something that did not make sense. Yomba gradually began to realize that her inability to sleep was not in vogue. It was anxiety. She was not *well*. All was not well with her and she had started to consider quitting, but for Abrema's voice that consistently rang in her head:

Jobs are very hard to find these days, you know. Why don't you stay there for a few more years and see what happens? For all you know, you are overreacting with this Madam Bose issue. Don't forget that you are paid well. Where are you going to get a job like this again?

Abrema was her maternal aunt who was not old enough to be an aunt, so she simply told everyone they were cousins. Abrema had completed university at the same time as Yomba. At some point during their stay in the university, they lived in the same room. It was always interesting to explain to their friends how they were cousins, yet one was an Nzema and the other a Gonja. *Legend* has it that Abrema was born when her father was in his eighties. Her mother was the fifth wife of Ekow Ackaah and Abrema was the fifteenth and last of his *known* children. Yomba's mother was the third out of fifteen but the first child of wife number two. Abrema moved to Accra to live with Yomba's mum, Sista Mondo, from the age of six when their father died. Her mother became a widow, and the family head had *ruled* that she would be unfit to take care of Abrema without the financial support of her dad, Ekow Ackaah. It was decided that since Esi had no real income, the last child of the family should be adopted by Sista Mondo who was, at the time, married and 'doing well' in the city of Accra. No consideration was given to Sista Mondo's own family situation – that she was pregnant expecting her second child or that she had a four-year-old daughter to take care of. She had very little choice. She accepted to 'adopt' her sister and became her guardian. It was Abrema who nicknamed her sister, *Sista Mondo*, when at the age of three, she was unable to fully pronounce 'Sister Mondoley'. When Abrema moved to Accra, everyone else caught on to using the nickname and it stuck.

Yomba had to resist the temptation to check her barrage of instant messages. She failed. Twitter was buzzing as usual – the word 'Joseph' was top of the trends. Someone had made a joke about people who ate cat meat as a delicacy in Ghana and wondered why it was called 'Joseph'. Then the 'Joseph' jokes started a trend. If there was one thing, she knew aggravated her *condition*, it was her trying to catch up with what was going on in the ever-busy world of social media. She could never catch up – there was always something that needed more time to figure out and there were the hundreds of messages from the WhatsApp chat groups she was in – one for her primary school, one for her junior high school, one for her immediate family and several for work. She had lost count of the number of groups – a good number of them she had muted – but she did not exit any of them because she did not want to have to explain anything to anyone.

Yomba wished she did not have to go back to work. Whoever made it a life rule that work had to be every week day was responsible for her misery. The weekends were short, and the weekdays were *super* long. She was not living her best life – as it had been portrayed when she was younger – *go to school, get good grades, get a job and enjoy life.* She was realizing that being an adult was hard work. She felt trapped. If she did not have to deal with the questions from her mother and her aunt, she would easily quit. Then, she would have to figure out the other critical matter – how to pay her bills. Being an adult came with bills, bills and more bills. She had moved out of her parents' home as soon as she got a permanent job. That is when she got introduced to the real world – the world of *bills*. If she could figure out how to pay her bills and buy all the things she bought without having to actually go to work, explaining to Abrema and Sista Mondo would be a breeze. They both thought that she was taking the blessing of finding a job, straight out of university, for granted and they never failed to remind her.

"Do you know that there is an association of unemployed graduates in Ghana? You have a job, keep it and stop whining," her mum had once said.

She will go to work and for the umpteenth time, be frustrated and depressed. She closed her eyes, tried to take her mind off what was coming in the morning and soon, sleep came calling.

****

Bose was the quintessential corporate executive. She had moved to Accra, Ghana, from her home country of Nigeria as an expatriate country manager in a multinational firm. She moved with her family – two children, eight-month-old Ama Funmilayo, four-year-old Kweku Babatunde and her husband, Dr. Mantse Laaye Mensah, who technically simply moved *back home*. He was Ghanaian. Mantse had been teaching Calculus at the University of Lagos, popularly known as 'Unilag', before moving back home with Bose.

When it was time to return after his doctoral studies, naturally, his family and friends assumed he would accept an offer to teach at the University of Cape Coast as it would offer him the opportunity to be in Ghana and in a city just about ninety minutes from his parents' home and his home town, 'British Accra'.

"Come back to Ghana and make sure you don't come with Amy," his sister, Naa, had said when they discussed his options. "Mantse, I know you like Amy very much, but there is no way she will fit into our family. So please don't bring her with you."

Mantse would always laugh and assure her that Amy will be fine wherever they chose to live and that is, *if* they were getting married.

"You're living with her and telling me *if* you get married? Are you not already married?" Naa asked sternly.

Naa and Mantse, had always been close, yet disagreed on almost everything yet they had just each other. Mantse chose, against Naa's advice, to go to Nigeria. He believed that if he went to Nigeria and Amy decided to move with him, they would be out of the prying eyes of family and they could live their lives in peace.

"Naa, thank you! I'll call you later in the day."

"You're welcome. I'll soon start charging you consultancy fees."

They exchanged a few more words and Mantse ended the call. He opened up his laptop, searched for the email from the University of Lagos and began to type:

Dear Prof. Rotimi,

Thank you for your email and the offer to join the faculty at your university. I would like to proceed with the discussion towards taking up a faculty position in September. I am available for a call at 2 pm Nigerian time. I look forward to your response.

Best regards,

Mantse.

Send.

He got up to get himself a cup of coffee; Amy was asleep. It was still quite early in Toronto, but he had woken up to speak to Naa. The time difference made communicating with his family in Ghana an interesting manoeuvring of time zones. He poured himself a cup of coffee from the coffee maker, sipped a bit of it and set the mug down. Amy hated it when he left his mug with the remaining contents sitting on the table instead of placing the mug in the sink, or simply rinsing it out and putting it back on the rack. He always feigned forgetfulness. This time he rinsed out the mug, set it on the kitchen counter, and went back into the bedroom snuggling up to Amy. He was grateful for many things and one of them was *his* Amy. Now, he was considering moving to Nigeria with her. That is, if she will agree to go along with him because he had not discussed with her *yet*. But, he was positive she will agree to move with him. At least, for the first few months and then they will see how things work out. They will discuss it in the morning… the morning when the sun is dancing in the sky, and they were both up.

Two months later, Mantse was on a plane heading to Lagos – the commercial capital of Nigeria, *alone*. Amy refused to move to Nigeria with him. She was not ready to move. Mantse had made up his mind. Long-distance relationships were not that difficult with the blessing of technology. They did not break up, but before he got on the flight to Lagos, he knew the lingering hug, and the tears at the airport, *was* goodbye. Forever. Six months after he left Toronto for Lagos, he met Bose.

Bose was the CEO of an Information Communication Technology (ICT) consultancy firm and they met by happenchance. He had been asked by his Head of Department to represent the department on a panel for a vendor presentation towards the award of a contract. He was not sure why they needed someone from the Mathematics department for that. Prof. Rotimi explained that the Procurement Committee of the Faculty of Science had a representative from each of the departments. The Head of Department was the designated representative, but he had grown weary of attending meetings of this nature and was, therefore, delegating Mantse to stand in for him. Mantse obliged.

He met Bose – elegant, eloquent and eccentric. She wore bright red-rimmed glasses and had her hair in natural twists. She spoke confidently and flawlessly and articulated, very fluidly, why her firm was the best option for the contract. Mantse looked at her without hearing a lot of what she was saying: he was fixated on something else. He liked her. He liked her personality and her drive. He looked at her intently. Taking in her presence, her poise.

After the presentation, they exchanged curt pleasantries and he left for his office. It was all he could do without coming across as a perverted university lecturer who wanted to use his position on the committee to get a woman. It was okay if he never saw her again, because he was not going to risk a scandal in his first year on the job.

However, fate had a different plan for him. A week after, he ran into her at the faculty's administration block. The glint in her eye confirmed that she knew him, or better put, she remembered him. There was no doubt about that, and it was inconsequential to ask if he, Mantse, remembered her. They became friends from that day, and she helped him settle into Lagos better by showing him around the Island. Bose was a Lagosian[2] and was raised in the heart of the city – *Isale Eko*. She was an alumna of the University of Lagos and had started her own company right after completing her youth service. She had been running it for a few years when she put in a bid for the Faculty of Science project. It took one month of back and forth and endless bureaucracy until the contract was awarded. When she received notice of the award of the contract through her email, only one person came to mind.

"Mantse, I got the contract! I got the contract!"

Mantse was happy for her but at the same time, he was not in the best of moods. He and Amy had just *officially* broken up. He was not surprised; it had been staring them in the face for a while. However, it hit hard because he was just not psyched at that particular moment to assimilate what this meant for him and a future he had created in his imagination. The distance had caused a strain on their relationship but more so, his inability to communicate when he would visit her within the next year was more of the bone of contention. Amy was happy he was settling in well, but

---

[2]A native or inhabitant of Lagos, Nigeria.

after hearing about Bose one too many times, she began to ask more questions. She was not wrong. Mantse was in love with his new friend, Bose. There was no denying it.

"I love you Mantse, but our relationship cannot survive like this. If you ever decide to come back to Canada, let me know. Maybe, I'll still be single and we can hook up again."

And this was Amy making light, a tense situation. She chose her words carefully and with each word, a sharp pain pierced his heart.

The call was the nail in the coffin, there was already a decaying corpse. The relationship died the minute Mantse sent the email to Professor Rotimi, accepting the position in Lagos without discussing it with Amy. She felt slighted that she was not consulted since this move involved the both of them. She felt Mantse was selfish with his decision and this was something she could not easily let go. They both knew it and yet, they remained in denial.

"This is great news, Bose. Congratulations."

"Mantse, what is wrong? Are you okay?"

"Amy broke up with me." The line went silent for a while.

"I'm so sorry, Mantse. Do you want to talk about it?"

"No, I don't want to rain on your parade. Let's talk tomorrow."

"Are you sure? I am not busy, we can talk."

"No, it's fine. I'll be fine."

"Okay, I'll call you in the morning. Good night Mantse."

"Good night Bose, congratulations again," and with these words, he ended the call. He needed to be alone to sort out his emotions and engaging Bose was, certainly, not ideal.

Eighteen months after Dr Mantse Laaye Mensah moved to Nigeria, he was getting married to Bose. Naa was his 'best woman' and dressed up appropriately to play the part. She wore a trouser-suit and a pair of crepe hoofs, *not* a dress and high-heeled pair of shoes. Both families were present to lend their support to the union. Everyone was happy, but none surpassed Mantse's. He had married his friend. He considered moving to Nigeria one of the best decisions he had made – if all he got out of it was meeting Bose. She was driven and fun to be around. He liked the fact that they could have long conversations about politics, the socio-cultural trends in Africa and what more, their tastes in music was very similar. Even though Bose was five years younger than Mantse, she seemed to have an older soul and her choice of music was evidence of it. She could sing all of Fela's songs, loved country music and idolized Bob Marley; yet, she was fast to dance along to a Davido song and was captivated by Tiwa Savage, Yemi Alade and Koredo Bello.

Mantse had secretly worshipped Fela but always felt identifying with his music was 'anti-intellectual'. So, whilst he could sing along to most of the songs on *Zombie*, Fela's 1976 album, Bose was the first person, outside his close circle of friends, to hear him sing. He had been particularly infatuated with Fela's ability to defiantly oppose the military regimes of his time and would always laugh at the lyrics of the title track, *Zombie*. How anyone was bold enough to sing about the military in that manner was what endeared Mantse to Fela Anikulapo Kuti. On one of their evenings together in his small lecturers' apartment, he surprised Bose by screaming the lyrics:

Go and kill! Joro, jaro, joro
Go and die! Joro, jaro, joro
Go and quench! Joro, jaro, joro
Put am for reverse! Joro, jaro, joro…

All the while, gyrating his waist and moving his legs vigorously in an attempt to mimic the pioneer of afrobeat music.

Mantse was born three years after the *Zombie* album was launched and was eighteen when Fela died. But he had interacted so much with his music, thanks to his father who was attracted to the struggle for equal rights and justice that was sweeping across Africa. This was in the late seventies and early eighties. He was a member of the generation that had chanted: "*Let the blood flow*", as the young Flight Lieutenant Jerry John Rawlings, leading the Armed Forces Revolutionary Council (AFRC), carried out a coup on 4th June 1979 and undertook a 'house cleaning' exercise that resulted in the execution of perceived corrupt military officers. He had later confided in Mantse:

"I don't think the revolution succeeded. We supported the military and people were executed, but we are back to the same corruption we wanted to purge our nation of," he had said. "I believe our good intentions did not translate into the nation we envisioned. Maybe we should never have broken free of colonialism."

That was always the point of a heated argument between Mantse and his almost seventy-year-old father. How could anyone think that colonialism was better than the current dispensation? True, there was corruption, but was colonialism not the rawest form of human degradation and rape of a people's dignity? Did colonialism not intimate that one race was more 'superior' to the other and, therefore, had a legitimate right to rule the 'inferior' race? Mantse's attempts rarely yielded much, but his father would always smile and quietly say, "Small boys are young".

****

Bose was nonchalant when she was first offered a job as Country Manager of a multinational distributor of computers and computer accessories. She had run her own business for 7 years and had become a key partner for Altimatum Computers Inc. in Nigeria. She consulted for them as they worked to develop an aggressive expansion plan across West Africa. One day, after a series of email exchanges, Teddy, the regional manager for Europe, Middle East and Africa, indicated that he would like to have a quick discussion with her over the phone.

"Would you be available to take a call from me in the next hour or so?" he wrote.

"Sure. I'll be in the office for another two hours, so you may call."

It was during that call that he popped the question.

"Bose, we need someone to lead our expansion plan across West Africa. We want you to do it."

Bose was silent for all of sixty seconds and then giggled loudly.

"Teddy, I am successfully running my consultancy. I do not have any intentions of letting go of my business."

"We are not asking you to let go of your business. We are simply asking you to join our team as Country Manager for Ghana and a few other West African countries, subsequently," Teddy responded.

"You don't have to give me a response now, you can take a few days to think about it and then we can talk."

"Perfect plan," Bose quipped.

"I will get back to you in a few days."

"Thank you, Bose."

"Thank you too, Teddy."

For Bose, this conversation ended with a boatload of anxiety and a tad of elation. She had never worked for anyone aside brief internships as an undergraduate and for her youth service. She had considered it in the early days of unemployment but once she started her firm, the desire to be employed vanished, completely. She was almost flattered that Teddy would ask her and then in between feeling flattered and happy, she began to feel inadequate.

What will happen if I am unable to achieve my goals? Would I be good at working in a large size organisation when I have run my own business of fewer than 10 employees all these years? What about if I don't like it after I start? Then what?

Thankfully, her voice of possibility whispered to her gently:

Bose, relax, you're overthinking this. Think about it carefully and then you can make a decision. Besides, if you start this and you don't like it, you can always return to your consulting work and get on with your life. And to not being good enough or of the possibility of you failing, forget that. You have successfully run this firm. Managing a small team even in a global firm won't be much different. Chill.

She had to discuss this with Mantse. But first, there was a pending issue she had to resolve. She had been putting this off for a while. She took a glance at her watch – 5:45 pm. She took her phone and dialled the number. Adaora picked on the first ring:

"Hey, you! I've been waiting for you to return my call all day! Nawa[3] for you o. So, you can't take a few minutes off your day to chat with me anymore. Is it that you're busy or…?"

"Adaora! I don call you now… How you dey?[4]"

"Abeg, make I hear word. Na so you just dey form say you be tycoon wey you no dey mind your friends again. Or, ebi say me I never marry so I no have anytin do?[5]"

"No now, na small busy I make[6]"

This went on for a while until they finally settled down to discuss the 'business of the day'.

Bose and Adaora had been friends for over twenty years. They went to the same senior high school and then the same university for undergraduate studies. Theirs was a very interesting friendship: it was considered an enigma to

---

[3] Pidgin: Wow or you have just blown me away

[4] Pidgin for: I have called you. How are you?

[5] Pidgin for: Please be quiet. Is it because you're now a business tycoon you no longer have time for your friends? Or, is it because I am not married, you assume I have nothing to do?

[6] Pidgin for: No, I've just been a bit busy

their wider network of friends. Bose was calm, intentional and purposeful. The one who never flunked any classes and always wanted to be on time for every meeting; Adaora was the complete opposite. She was the life of the party; the only child of a wealthy businesswoman who controlled a significant portion of the commercial activity in Onitsha. From an early age, she was treated like a princess and by the time she was heading off to university, her friends had nicknamed her 'Adaeze', meaning King's daughter.

Even though she did not like the nickname, it stuck. So, when they jokingly called out to her: "Adaeze", she will respond, waving her hand in the air, "my people". It was this penchant to attract attention to herself that made her character a sharp contrast to that of Bose. Bose rarely showed up amid a large crowd. Although she was quite eloquent in her class discussions and considered one of the brightest students, she was not a 'regular' at social events except those Adaora forced her to attend.

So, what was it that bound Adaora and Bose? They could not put a finger to it, but they were best friends and keeping in touch with each other was getting more difficult as life evolved for them both. Adaora was running her mother's business across three large cities – Onitsha, Port Harcourt and Lagos and Bose was growing her business from scratch, a feat that seemed almost impossible to her when she first started. She was thankful they could stay in touch and catch up, even though it was getting more and more infrequent. What made it special, however, was that no matter how long it took for them to get back together, it always seemed they just picked up from where they last left off.

After a hearty chat that seemed to never end, the phone call ended with Bose promising to be available to have lunch with Adaora when she was next in Lagos. Her conversations with Adaora were usually a combination of 'gist', Adaora whining about how she hated having to deal with her uncles and a discussion on what they were each doing to get ahead in life. Bose liked Adaora – she was a sounding board; she was her friend.

It was time to head home. Thankfully, she did not work far from home. Unlike a few of her friends who worked on the Island but lived on the mainland, she did not have to contend with the Third Mainland Bridge and *hold up*[7]. Mantse was not that lucky. Teaching at the University of Lagos meant that he had to commute across town about four times a week. Thankfully, he did not have to drive during rush hour traffic and had the luxury to spend the night on campus in his modest lecturer's apartment if he felt a need to work late into the night. He rarely did and always joked about how that apartment made him feel like a bachelor. He did not like the coldness of the bed without Bose.

"It is not the apartment you don't like; it is because you will not be able to find anything on your own if you lived alone *jare*[8]," Bose would jest in response.

---

[7] Nigerian slang that means heavy traffic

[8] Yoruba word for *please*

It had been a packed week for her and she was looking forward to a relaxing weekend. She also had to decide on Teddy's proposal. *No pressure,* she told herself.

"No be me kill Jesus,[9]" she said out loud as if in response to someone else.

---

[9]Pidgin for: I did not kill Jesus. To wit: I can relax.

CHAPTER TWO

Beads of sweat had begun to break out on her brow. She had been on this route a couple of times but each time, she went on the same emotional roller coaster. Three years ago, she experienced her first real air travel scare. Ten minutes into a flight from Lagos to Accra, the pilot announced that they were approaching thunderstorms. It felt pretty routine until the plane began to bounce like a yo-yo and with each downward motion, Yomba knew this was *it*. She never recovered from that. But she never told anyone. At least once a quarter, she had to go to Nigeria to meet with clients or prospects. She endured the flight every single time.

She closed her eyes and tried to even out her breath. Being in a window seat did not help matters so she shut the blind. After about what seemed like the longest two minutes, the plane stabilized, and the pilot's voice could be heard over the PA system. She was not paying attention.

"Are you okay?" he asked.

It was only then that she realized she has been holding onto the arm of a stranger. She let go of his arm, quite embarrassed and said in a faint, almost inaudible voice, "I'm okay."

Well, thank God for friendly strangers, she thought to herself.

Chidi had caramel brown skin and so her grip had caused his arm to redden a bit and Yomba tried not to look at his arms, almost embarrassed that she had caused it. Chidi smiled at her and revealed wonderful dentition. He was gently rubbing his arm, as if to soothe away the redness. She wanted to reach out, touch his arm and apologize. However, she stopped herself because he was a *stranger* and did not want her gesture to be misinterpreted. As the blood rushed to her face, her cheeks grew warm. More in response to the beautiful smile Chidi flashed her way, than the reddened hand of a total stranger. Or, was it just the after-effect of her panic? This thought jolted her back into the awareness of her surroundings. Her heart began to race.

So, it is not enough that you have bruised the guy's arm, you like him too? Calm down, girl. This is not what you're thinking. Besides, it was just a smile and maybe, he was smiling because you finally let go of his arm. A smile of relief. That's it. Nothing more.

"I am Chidi, what's your name?" Chidi broke into her racing thoughts.

Is he talking to me? Oh, after I've embarrassed myself by being so scared. No, he is not talking to me.

"Were you here for work or pleasure?" He added.

He is talking to me.

"Hi. I'm Yomba. I had a business meeting here and I'm heading back home."

Does anyone come to Lagos for pleasure? She wondered.

"That's good to know. I'm off to Accra to spend some time with my family. It's my first time. I hope I'll like it."

He's married? Ah! So much for a handsome stranger.

"Well, Accra isn't as busy as Lagos and it's a lot calmer. I'm sure you will enjoy it!"

At this point, she was ready to continue her flight in silence. She was not going to indulge this handsome *married* man.

But if he is married, how come his family lives in Accra and it is his first time? That does not add up.

She adjusted her seat and momentarily closed her eyes, a gesture that prompted Chidi to believe that she wanted to end the conversation.

"Can I take your number? I'm sure having a friend in Accra won't be a bad idea. Maybe when I need a break from babysitting my twin nieces, you can show me around?"

Whew! He isn't married.

"Sure, I'll be happy to. My number is…"

****

It had been two weeks since he arrived in Accra and was beginning to feel sad. He was not sure if it was the fact that he was going back to the highly pressurized life of his bank job that made him sad, or that he was going to miss Yomba. They had grown quite close since meeting on the flight and to him, it seemed weird that they could be so close after just two weeks. It was too fast!

Maybe, he should move to Ghana and find a job? Or maybe, he could ask for a transfer from his office? After all, his company had recently expanded into Ghana. The expansion into Ghana was their Founder and CEO's grand plan to make the bank a leader in West Africa. But why Ghana? Ghana was such a small country with a population just a little under the population of Lagos State. It had been a big internal debate in the bank and the majority of the staff felt that the plan was dead on arrival. But the 'powers that be' had decided and to Ghana, they came.

Their bank happened to be one of five Nigerian banks that had set up shop in Ghana. After three years, the move had turned out to be quite successful. Even though the naysayers had given the plan eighteen months to fall through, it had begun to look positive within twelve months, thanks to an ambitious customer-driven approach. The stories of what they had achieved in twelve months had spread throughout the bank like wildfire, and the team in Ghana was hailed as being the 'game changers' for the bank. The thought of joining the team in Ghana because he wanted to be close to Yomba did not seem like a bad idea at all. At least, she will be around to help him settle in and be his escape from the drudgery.

"Uncle Chidi! Uncle Chidi!" his niece, Gracie, was tugging at his trouser, trying to get his attention.

"Yes, Gracie." He scooped her up in his arms and whirled her around

"Again, Uncle Chidi. Again!"

Gracie was his four-year-old niece. Her twin sister, Gloria, was fast asleep on the sofa but Gracie seemed to never settle down. Babysitting these two was a full-time job and not what he wanted to be doing on a Saturday afternoon. But he loved them and was happy to be able to spend some time with them. His sister, Nene, had moved to Ghana to take up a role as the Human Resource Manager for a shipping company. She arrived in Ghana, four months pregnant, with her husband in tow. She had worked with the firm in Nigeria for five years as an HR Business Partner and was at that point where she needed a change. When the opportunity to take up a regional managerial role in Ghana presented itself, the least of her worries was her pregnancy. She said *yes* before even thinking about it. Before leaving Nigeria, she discussed her medical options with her doctor and was given a file with all of her records. She knew she was having twins and she was travelling to a country she had never been to.

"Nene, isi o mebiri gi?[10]" her mother screamed. "I am old. I will not be there to help you. You don't know anyone there. How will you manage?"

Nene had anticipated the opposition and had a prepared speech for her parents. What she did not expect was her father's support.

"Amaka, she will be fine. De people wey dem dey born for Ghana wey dema mama no dey, how den dey take manage?[11]"

Nene's mother looked at him in utter bewilderment. This man was simply a bundle of contradictions. He was the same man who proclaimed: "Over my dead body will a

---

[10] Ibo: translated as: "Are you crazy?" Ibo is the principal native language of the Ibo people, an ethnic group of South Eastern Nigeria.

[11] Pidgin for: Amaka, she will be fine. The people who give birth to children in Ghana and do not have their mothers with them, how do they cope?

child of mine marry and bear fruits with an *osu*! None will associate with any member of that accursed tribe". And this was the outburst that met Nene when she brought home an '*osu*"[12] and informed her family she was getting married to him.

Nene had no idea who an *osu* was and after being in a relationship with Emeka since their second year in University, they had decided to legalize their union. Their friends already called them *Mr and Mrs Emeka*. As far as Nene was concerned, after being together for six years, she was going to marry Emeka, with or without her parents' consent. Emeka, on the other hand, got scared when Nene told him about what her father said. Emeka had grown up in Lagos, far away from the culture of his ethnic group, and his parents had never broached the subject. He went to his parents' home that weekend and asked them about the *osu* castes and why was it that he had never been told about this?

"It is irrelevant, outmoded and a very primitive thing that happened decades ago. I married your father and defied the so-called caste system. If Nene has any sense, she will marry you in a hurry."

His mother was very calm about the matter, a direct contrast to Nene's weeping when she narrated her encounter

---

[12] An osu is a member of the **Osu caste**, an ancient practice across Ibo land which strongly bars any social interaction and marriage between the diala (free-born) and osu (outcast) whose progenitors were believed to have been enslaved or dedicated to the deities of a community or village.

with her father. Emeka had his parents blessing and Nene decided she was going to rebel. One week to their set date, Nene's parents called her and agreed, reluctantly, to support her. Not without letting her know that the consequences of her decisions lay solely at her feet and that of her children. Despite how insensitive Nene thought that was, it was more than enough for her because, finally, she had their *disguised* blessing to marry her Emeka.

Mama Chidi shook her head in wonder. She couldn't believe that this same man was fine with his only daughter going to Ghana. *Moving to Ghana* for a job with a pregnancy and no idea how she was going to take care of her unborn babies... twins! She turned and stared at her husband again, who, even though was seated and contributing to their conversation, was also paying attention to a news story on TV.

"Mama, I will be fine. And who says you can't come to Ghana? I will buy a ticket for you to visit me and the children. Don't worry."

"I will be so happy to visit Ghana: the land of Kwame Nkrumah and the great Asante Kotoko," her father said.

"So, you will go and help her take care of her children, abi[13]?" Mama Chidi asked.

"No now! I will follow you to go and help her, my dear wife."

---

[13] Pidgin: *Abi* – is it true? The Osu has been described as "sacred slavery" and even though there are now laws abolishing all forms of discrimination, there are reports of this practice being in existence

Papa Chidi said, in his best matter-of-factly voice which drew laughter from all present.

Serendipity is what Chidi called the whole situation now. If Nene had not moved here, he would not have met Yomba and he would not be thinking about moving jobs to be close to his new *friend*. Friend? Was she *just* his friend? Well, so far, they had spent every Sunday, since he arrived, together and they had endless text conversations. They started texting each other in the morning, as soon as Yomba got into her office, typically about 8 am, and will talk through the day via text, discussing various things. Chidi looked forward to hearing from her every single day and under the short span of their friendship, he felt he had a real connection with her. He knew all her colleagues. Well, at least, the ones she worked closely with.

There was *Shine-Shine Boy* – Kwame – who dressed very well and pretended to be a star performer in the sales team. *Drama Queen,* Akosua – "emotionally unstable" is how Yomba described her. She would rush into the washroom and cry after every Monday meeting when she was not achieving her targets and did not want to discuss her difficulties with anyone but Yomba. She felt the office was laden with devilish people who wanted to 'steal her glory'. Then there was Bose! Bose was Yomba's biggest nightmare: the Country Manager who was never satisfied with anything Yomba did. Bose was Nigerian, just like Chidi, and that made the situation worse. Every single time Yomba talked about her, she would add, "That your Naija sister..." Chidi hid his irritation a few times but let it out on one such occasion when Yomba's generalization tugged on some raw nerves.

"I have only one sister and her name is Nene. Is every Ghanaian in Nigeria your sister or brother? How come you do not refer to Dangote, Africa's richest man, as my Naija brother?" he quipped.

Yomba could not help laughing. Her laughter was like music to his ears. He had never heard anyone laugh so heartily, so pure and without restraint. Her laughter was more like a cachinnation: the kind that made you want to look around the room and wonder who was gaping at you and your friend. She was unrestrained and free when she laughed. He liked that very much. And though he might have been a bit irritated earlier, whenever she laughed, he laughed too.

In five days, he will return to Lagos and to his regular life – where laughter was rare and long days of texting were considered taboo. How could he, when he left his phone in his laptop bag for long stretches at a go. His job as a credit analyst required a lot of detailed due diligence and he had grown accustomed to working in silence; thus, he considered his phone a major distraction. Well, that will have to change. He was not going to give up this new habit for anything – not even for all the pounded yam and ogbono soup in his mother's kitchen. That was in the future. For now, he was going to concentrate on Gracie and Gloria and later, in another few hours, he will be with his *friend* – Yomba.

CHAPTER THREE

When Bose arrived at home, Babatunde (Tunde) could be heard from outside, crying. Bose glanced at her watch – 6:30 pm. It was bath time and, typically, Tunde always had a reason why he did not want to take his bath in the evening. His nanny would have to coax and cajole him but that usually took a few minutes of snotty-nosed crying and Mantse always came to the nanny's rescue by speaking to Tunde. Bose figured something else must be wrong because Tunde's bellows were unusually loud for a child who simply did not want to take a bath. She walked in through the front door and saw Tunde lying on his back crying. He took a glance in his mother's direction and calmed down just enough to get up and run into her arms.

"Kí ló n se é"?[14]" she asked. Tunde was sobbing quietly now.

"Madam, please he did not finish his dinner so I turned off the TV and told him to finish so we can go and bath. That is why he is crying," said Lucy, the nanny.

---

[14] Translated as: "What is wrong with you" in Yoruba. Yoruba is the principal language of the Yoruba people, an ethnic group in the Southwestern part of Nigeria.

"Oh, my dear, you didn't eat, and you want to watch TV? Let's go and finish the food for mummy and then we will bath quickly and come and watch, okay?" Bose said, trying to placate Tunde. He nodded as his mother walked him to the table.

Funmi was the baby, but she was so much calmer than Tunde. During the raucous, she was calmly sucking away at her finger whilst asleep in the corner of the living room. How she could sleep when Tunde was crying did not make much sense to Bose, especially since she was almost always awakened by the voices of her parents when they walked into a room. Bose's theory was that Funmi slept to drown out Tunde's noise-making but loved the presence of her parents.

After about ninety minutes, the house was quiet – Funmi and Tunde were sound asleep. Mantse had emerged from the study where he had been on a video call with a student he was remotely supervising. He could hear Tunde's cries, but it was not loud enough to distract him, so he tried to drown him out and continue. Bose's arrival was *so* welcome as the situation got better almost immediately – talk of perfect timing. He was able to complete the discussions peacefully without wondering what his son was up to. He was not sure which made him more stressed – the crying of his son, or the nanny who could not resolve the situation without the direct intervention of one of Tunde's parents?

"Hey!"

"Hey!"

Mantse reached out to his wife and hugged her. She hugged him back and lingered for a moment. Keeping her head in the pocket of his neck.

"How was your day?" he asked.

She spoke directly into his ears.

"It was okay. I had a good day." She pulled away and began to head for the sofa. She lay down in the spot she would most likely fall asleep.

"I had a chat with Teddy. They've offered me a role in Ghana."

Mantse was slightly out of earshot as he had walked into the kitchen to get water. He returned with two glasses.

"What did Teddy say?" Mantse asked as he handed her the extra glass of water he was holding. With this, Bose was compelled to repeat what she just said.

"What do you want to do? Moving to Ghana won't be a bad idea at all. I'm just not sure about your giving up your company and what you've built here," he replied with concern.

They had a long conversation and it seemed like a good opportunity, but there were sacrifices to be made, especially for Mantse, who was now fully tenured at the university. This move would require he finds a new job in Ghana.

"Well, I am due for sabbatical leave. Let me take the leave and see how things go," he said, feigning sadness. It was obvious to him that Bose wanted to take the job and he was not going to stand in her way. They began to discuss the move and her excitement was infectious.

Secretly, Mantse was happy. He had been longing for a change of environment. The timing had to be right, though. They will have to plan it to sync with the academic calendar. Exams in May, grading due by the middle of July and he would be ready to leave by the middle of August. Being on sabbatical leave meant he will have enough time to help the children settle into a new school. They had three months clear to wind down and make the move. They decided – Bose will hand over the running of her consultancy to one of her partners with a special contract which included profit sharing. After 12 months, they will re-evaluate the terms and discuss an extension if necessary.

Bose opened her laptop and created an excel sheet and named it: 'Ghana Move'. She listed all the things they had to figure out before they moved and the timelines they were considering. Then she opened up her email and sent an email to Teddy:

Hello Teddy,

Let's discuss an offer relating to the job opportunity we discussed earlier today. You can send me details of the role, the compensation package and all necessary information for me to take a look. Once I've taken a look at it, we can talk.

I'll look forward to your response.

Regards,

Bose

She hit send.

She was already half asleep but wanted to catch up on the evening news and what was going on in *Trump-land*. No sooner had she turned on the TV than she fell asleep. It seemed the turning on the television was now her fastest way to *la-la land*. Mantse always had to wake her up and sometimes, it was a daunting task for him. This time, he just allowed her to sleep and changed the channel to watch a movie.

Life is too stressful to spend the evening watching CNN bash Donald Trump all evening, he thought.

Come to think of it, Mantse mused, this was the decade of a lot of interesting happenings like one unfolding movie plot: Barack Obama, the United States of America's first African-American president had served two terms and been succeeded by someone who was considered a political *outsider* – Donald Trump; Kim Jong-un was the *supreme leader* of North Korea and an interesting relationship between North Korea, the US and Russia was unfolding. Kim Jong-un had been fondly nicknamed, 'rocket man', by Donald Trump. Muhammadu Buhari, who he had read about in his West African history class as a president of Nigeria in the 80s, was president *again* and serving his second term in office. Sebastian Kurz was the youngest world leader at thirty-two years old, as chancellor of Austria. Ghana was in an election year that would see, for the first time, a former president – John Dramani Mahama, run for office with the prospect of serving only one term. He had lost a second term bid to the current President and was seeking a return. The world had a lot going on! And there would be a lot to explain to his children in the next couple of years, including Elon Musk's electric cars and Richard Branson's space tourism. Explaining the many innovations that the era of digitization had brought about would not be much of an issue as they will grow up with it as second nature. His major concern was with all the other things it came with.

Well, for now, he was simply going to watch a Nollywood movie, relax and enjoy a quiet evening. All things being equal, in another few months, he will be home in Ghana on sabbatical leave. *Sabbatical.* What a lovely word. Essentially, he will still be employed by the university, get paid and have enough time to explore and decide on his next move.

****

Chidi had not been one to look forward to Sundays. His earliest memories of Sunday mornings were of his mother screaming at him to hurry up and get ready for morning mass. As a teenager, he had rebelled and decided he was no longer going to keep up with waking up so early on a Sunday just to go and doze off in church. Sleeping in the church was not the issue. It was the stone-cold treatment his mother gave him after mass that made him so uncomfortable.

"The devil has captured your heart and so you can't stay awake in church, abi?" She had once said.

How could he stay awake when he had been out all night, snuck in at 2:00am and yet, was expected to be ready for mass at 7:30am? His father rarely went anyway; why could he not stay at home too? One Sunday, when his mother came storming into his room, he just turned and told her stoically:

"Mama, I am not going. I want to sleep. Going to church na by force?[15]"

He turned, pretending to be asleep, but expecting his mother's veracious response which, in earlier years, would have been accompanied by a whack with her wrapper or a flying slipper. He expected it... two seconds, five seconds, ten seconds and there was nothing. He turned to look, and his mother had walked away. He had won *finally*.

---

[15]Pidgin: Is going to church by force?

That was not the end. When he moved out of home at the age of twenty-three, his mother made it a point to call him every Saturday evening to check in on his wellbeing but, primarily, to remind him to go to mass on Sunday. On one such occasion, he had lied he went the previous week. Unfortunately, he was unprepared for the next line of questioning:

"What did the priest say, Chidi?"

He was caught totally off guard and fumbled with his response.

"Chidi you dey lie abi?[16] If you don't go to church and pray to God, how do you expect God to bless you?"

But, this was a different Sunday. Today, he was looking forward to church because it happened to be the place he would meet Yomba. Imagine his surprise when she mentioned she attended the same church as Nene. The prospect of attending church every week whilst he was in Ghana just looked so much brighter. Nene did not have to threaten to call Mama; Nene did not have to remind him on Saturday evening. Nene did not have to do anything. Yomba was his motivation.

The message from Pastor Mimi was quite resounding. He enjoyed the music in church and appreciated that the people he met who had so warmly embraced Nene and

---

[16]Pidgin for "You are lying, right?"

Emeka into their community. Pastor Mimi was an associate pastor and was preaching in the absence of the senior pastor. She preached on the topic: "What is in your hands?" This sermon spoke to Chidi. He had been wondering where his life was heading with the bank job everyone knew he loathed, and as it stood now, he was courting the idea of moving to Ghana. The biblical case study of Moses' interaction with God in Exodus Chapter 4 was the central scripture, but it was the connection to small beginnings that enticed his thoughts.

He had heard this bible story several times, but no one ever linked it to him starting on his dreams from the smallness of what he had *now*.

Did he have a talent? Was he naturally good at anything? he mused.

"Pray that the Holy Spirit will guide you to discover what your purpose is. Pray that you will have a fresh sense of purpose and the willingness to walk in that purpose. Pray that whatever confusion you have experienced about your purpose will be removed, in Jesus' name. Pray…"

Pastor Mimi led the congregation through a short time of prayer and then, the service gradually wound to a close.

****

"Hey Handsome!" she quipped, then almost bit her tongue when she realized she just spat out those words: *Hey handsome?* Where was that coming from? Maybe from the many stolen glances from the other end of the auditorium throughout the church service. Pastor Mimi's sermon had just washed over her this time. It was not her fault that Chidi was so *handsome* – but not as handsome as her *forever crush,* RMD,[17]" she thought and gently smiled to herself.

"Hello," replied Chidi, almost uncomfortable with the initial greeting referring to him as 'Handsome'.

He hugged her for what felt like the longest one minute, or was it ten seconds or even less? He quickly took in her fragrance and then withdrew from the embrace as fast as he had started it. After all, they were standing in the lobby of a busy charismatic church and Nene and Emeka were just an earshot away. He was going to have lunch with Yomba anyway and then, he will hug her for *real.* Today he had plans. It was his last week in Accra and he was going to make the best of it.

Chidi grabbed Yomba's hand and headed in the direction of Nene and Emeka. As they approached, Nene's face lit up. Chidi and Yomba looked so good together, but she also felt their relationship was doomed to fail… that is, if they were in a relationship or going to be in a relationship or thinking about being in a relationship – it will *fail.* Chidi was

---

[17]RMD is the initials for Richard Mofe-Damijo a celebrated Nigerian actor and former Commissioner for Culture and Tourism for Delta State, Nigeria

not the settling type and Yomba was too excited about her brother, who she knew was just not capable of focusing on one woman. It was not that he was a *Casanova*; it was just that in their teenage years, Chidi had always clearly articulated why he believed that the modern construct of monogamy was *"Unnatural, forced and a western cultural construct that an Ibo man like me cannot easily adapt to"*. Nene always laughed at the tone with which he described himself as *an Ibo man*.

"Is Papa not an Ibo man? Does he not have one wife?" Nene once asked.

Chidi laughed. The kind of laughter that made Nene feel very uncomfortable. He laughed in a way that said to Nene: *You have no clue of what you are saying.*

"What is so funny, Chidi? Does Papa not have only one wife?"

"Nothing is funny, Nene. I am just saying, that monogamy is not possible."

Chidi then quickly changed the subject but Nene had never forgotten that very sarcastic laugh that erupted when she referred to her father having only one wife. Maybe, he knew something she did not know. If he did, she did *not* want to know.

She was smiling at her brother and his friend, Yomba, and praying that Yomba gets to know of his ideology before they start anything. She will hate that a promising young lady will get entangled with her *polygamy-believing* brother.

"Good morning Nene and Emeka."

"Good morning Yomba."

Nene and Yomba hugged briefly. It was an awkward hug because Chidi was holding on to one of Yomba's hands as if his life depended on it and she had a clutch in the other hand.

"We are leaving church now. I will ride with Yomba and see you guys back in the house," Chidi explained with a wink.

He did not have to explain *again*. It was the third time he was reminding Nene, since they started off to church earlier on in the morning and on every single occasion, Emeka had snickered.

"That's fine. We will see you at home. Don't forget to bring me a pack of kelewele[18] from wherever you got it the last time."

"Yes ma," Chidi teased whilst pulling Yomba away.

"Nene, Emeka, please give my love to the children. I will see you later," Yomba said over her shoulders as she was gently dragged away.

[18]Popular Ghanaian meal - fried spiced ripe plantain.

Chidi only let her go when they got to her car and she needed to take the car key out of her clutch. *Today he is acting unusual,* she thought. Chidi was acting very clingy. *Ah well, maybe I'm overthinking this.*

Yomba opened the car, they both sat and strapped themselves in. Though Chidi was not a fan of seatbelts, he knew Yomba would not move till he was securely strapped.

"Chidi, what do you want to do today? Brunch, mall, movies…?" Yomba inquired as she turned to look at him.

"I don't want to do anything; I want to sleep."

"Oh, then should I drive you home?" she asked, trying hard to mask the tinge of disappointment that accompanied her words.

"No, no! I didn't mean it that way." *You did not mean it that way?* he thought to himself. "I meant; I don't want to be outdoors today. I want to spend the day with you. *Alone.* It is my last weekend here. Can we go to your place, maybe watch a movie and I'll make you brunch at home?"

Make me brunch at home?

Is this guy for real?

No way!

She had heard about this classic approach to a guy getting into a girl's bed. She was not having any of it. He visits you, tries to cook, you end up doing most of it and then he wants sex. *Sex!* The thought of it with Chidi made her feel very warm. She unconsciously shifted in her chair and turned the air-conditioning on even though the ignition was off. She did not want to have sex with him, at least, not now. She had just met him, and he was going back to Lagos in four days. Then what? Were the trips she made to Nigeria once a quarter good enough to sustain their relationship? *Relationship?* Was that what was happening here? No, she will not invite Chidi to her house. He had been there once already – just casually – on their way to the mall on his first Sunday. She needed to change clothes and had to do a quick stop at her house. Thankfully, her cousin, Abrema, was home so she was not left alone with Chidi. Today was different. Today she *hoped* Abrema will be away *forever.* She liked the prospect of spending the day with Chidi alone. But she also knew she did not want to allow what she knew will happen to happen. She will not allow it.

No visit. Plain and simple.

"Sure! I have enough food. You won't have to cook, and we can watch something on Netflix. Thankfully, Abrema is away today and tomorrow. She is spending time with her mum. So, we will be alone."

She gasped as she could not believe the words that just left her mouth.

Girl! You're playing with fire. Fire burns!

"Great! Let's go. Even if you have enough food, I'm happy to cook something for you. I'm the bonafide genius at using nothing to make lunch. I've lived alone for long enough to hone that skill."

"That sounds good," Yomba responded as she started the car and headed in the direction of her flat.

Chidi leaned slightly back in his chair. He liked the excitement in Yomba's voice as she agreed to his very modest plans. But more so, he liked that she was willing to commit her dietary wellbeing to him. He silently prayed, *"Lord, help me make a good impression on this lady"*. They travelled for most of the journey in silence as they listened to the serenading voice of Felix Van Persie on Cool FM.

CHAPTER FOUR

The negotiation between Bose and her new employers was swift but rigorous: Altimatum wanted her to join the team, and they wanted her to join *now*. Teddy was at the forefront of the negotiation and Bose felt comfortable dealing with him instead of their Director of Human Resources – Sylvia McDery. Their first encounter was not very pleasant and try as she could, Bose just could not get beyond Sylvia's cold emailing tone and her 'we-are-doing-you-a-favour' attitude. Eventually, Teddy, noticing the hostility between the two women, subtly took over the exchanges and Bose was appreciative.

They finally agreed. Bose, who had never had to negotiate compensation packages with a company, was particularly concerned about the stated three months 'notice period' Altimatum wanted included in the employment contract. *Three months!* Teddy tried to explain to her that for a country manager role, they wanted to protect themselves from the unlikely event that she decided to up and leave. Granted she may decide to move on at some point, but they wanted enough time to transition to a new person, communicate appropriately to their investors and plan a proper exit. It made sense, a lot of it. If they decided to terminate the contract, they will have to pay her three months' salary. All kosher!

She was scheduled to start in three months. Enough time to change her mind if she wanted to and enough time to wind down in Lagos, hand over the business to capable hands and then move to Ghana. The timing also worked for Mantse. He could end the academic year at the university and proceed on his much-deserved sabbatical leave.

Move to Ghana. Mantse was going to be close to his family and she was going to start a new job. The decision felt like the right thing to do but was she sure she would be able to succeed in *Ghana?*

"What was different about succeeding in Ghana?"

"Well, for starters, I do not know the terrain and I don't have friends in Ghana. No network. No mentors. No family."

"No family?" Mantse twirled to face her, obviously hurt by her words. "What am I to you? A stranger?"

She laughed.

"You know that's not what I meant."

She hugged him when she realized he was a bit upset. Then after a few seconds, he hugged her back and she held on as if her life depended on it.

"You will be just fine, my dear. We will be fine!" Mantse stated emphatically.

That was the conversation she had with Mantse the night before she signed the contract. It was all the assurance she needed to go ahead with this next phase. She continued to feel inadequate and wondered how she will fit into a different country, a different culture and succeed.

Ah well, what the heck? If it doesn't work, I will return to my consultancy in Lagos. Simple as ABC.

****

The move to Ghana was smooth. Their family and friends in Lagos, after the initial "Don't move to Ghana" choruses were very supportive. Even her friend, Adaora, spent a weekend in Lagos with them helping her pack up the things they needed for the initial move. That was after a long 'fight' over the phone.

"So na now you just dey tell me, abi? Now, wey you don decide finish. You sef, which kind friend you be?[19]" Adaora had quizzed.

---

[19]Pidgin: So, you are just telling me? When you have already made the decision. What kind of friend are you anyway?

"Sorry, Adaora. Na forget I forget. No be sey I no wan tell you.[20]"

Bose lied. She had not forgotten. She was afraid Adaora will discourage her and she did not want to allow herself to back out of the decision. So, she kept the news to herself until it was a month to go. By then, she had 'fortified' her explanations and was ready for anyone who had questions. Interestingly, Adaora did not discourage her.

"But Ghana sha, I hear say Ghana be fine place o. No, be this our Naija wey everything just scata finish. O girl! I dey happy for you o. So, me too I go talk sey, I have a friend for Ghana![21]"

They both erupted in a burst of thunderous laughter. Adaora was being modest. She had visited Ghana on a number of occasions and had even intimated she was considering buying a house there – Adaora, the business tycoon.

A few weeks after that call, she was in Lagos, helping her friend pack the last of what needed to be packed. Well, her plan was to help Bose pack, but she spent most of the time they had chatting away about her family business and the troubles she was having with one of her uncles who managed one of her mother's businesses. Everything she asked him to do to ensure sustainability was dismissed under the guise of "business no be about book long[22]".

---

[20] Pidgin: I forgot; it isn't that I didn't want to tell you.

[21] Pidgin: I hear Ghana is a nice place. Not like Nigeria where everything is chaotic. Girl! I'm happy for you. So, I'll also be able to say I have a friend in Ghana!

[22] Pidgin: Business is not about being intellectual

He had been in business for many years and still wanted to operationally manage the business like it has been done twenty-five years ago when he started it out with his big sister, Adaora's mother. He simply drove her crazy. Adaora was working to develop structures and operational efficiency across all their businesses. Her mother had given her blessings and stepped away from the operational side of things to allow her only daughter, a first-generation graduate, to develop what she believed will help the business. Unfortunately, everyone else was giving her a hell of a time. There was this one lady who worked with them and had been with them since day one, who used to refer to her as 'Baby Adaora'. She, a distant relative, had helped Adaora's mother, then a single mother starting a business in boisterous Onitsha, to take care of Adaora. Adaora was not a baby any longer and their business was not a small shop. After enduring being called 'Baby Adaora' in front of some customers one day, she pulled the older woman aside and stated firmly: "Aunty Chika, please, call me Adaora. That is my name. Not Baby Adaora." She did not give Aunty Chika any time to react; she walked into her office and shut the door. Aunty Chika did not mention her name again from that point on. She had a theory that Aunty Chika simply decided to pretend she did not exist and since they rarely had to work together, Adaora could care less.

"Maybe, I should just leave the business for them to run it as they want. I don taya.[23]"

---

[23] Pidgin: I am tired

Adaora rarely sounded defeated, but this time she did and that really surprised Bose.

"Adaora, since when you don start dey taya for anytin?[24]"

She looked at her friend and noticed something she had not seen in a very long time – Adaora was on the verge of tears.

"Bose, I don taya for my people o.[25]" Bose wrapped her arms around her friend as she broke into tears. This was very unusual. The only other time Bose had witnessed Adaora cry was when her grandfather had passed away and she had been informed whilst they were on campus. She was close to her grandfather, who had been very supportive of Adaora's mother when she had fallen pregnant as a teenager.

Contrary to the norm of the time, her grandfather had not compelled his daughter to marry the father of her child. He had defied the community and decided to raise his grandchild in his household and vowed that his grandchild will have his full support and blessing. His only concern was how his daughter, a child herself, could raise and support a child.

When he died, it was like Adaora had lost her lifetime hero, the only male figure in her life who made her feel safe and that was the first and only time Bose had seen Adaora cry. This time, Adaora was crying for a different reason:

---

[24]Pidgin: "Since when did anything make you fed up?"

[25]Pidgin: "I am tired of my people"

exhaustion, frustration and anger. Bose allowed her to cry for a few minutes.

"You go chop?[26]" Bose asked when her crying subsided.

Adaora laughed gently. Nothing will make her miss a good 'Bose-meal'.

They spent the rest of the evening talking about life and everything *but* their work. Bose was happy Mantse had taken the children out. She enjoyed the time alone with Adaora, even though they had achieved very little in terms of packing, she was happy. She had her friend with her. Life was good.

****

Yomba and Chidi had arrived at Yomba's flat. Chidi was left alone to take in the simple, yet classy ambience of the medium-sized flat. Yomba had a place for everything, making him feel uneasy about touching anything. But something caught his eye almost immediately: Yomba had a collection of miniature bronze images. They were possibly up to a dozen pieces arranged nicely on a centrepiece in the living room. These *Benin bronzes*, as they were called, were historically significant to Nigerians, but particularly the people of southern Nigeria. He was surprised his Ghanaian friend had a collection in her home. Yomba walked into the living room in time to catch the look of curiosity on his face.

---

[26] Pidgin for: Do you want to eat something?

"I see you've met my bronze army," she said.

"Yes. Where did you get them from? It is a bit strange for a young lady to have an attachment to these pre-colonial artefacts. Or are you a reincarnated spirit?" he queried jokingly.

Yomba laughed. Her laughter was always belly-deep and raucous.

"I got them as a gift from an Aunty of mine who lives in Warri. She gave them to me as a gift when I completed my first degree with a first-class. She handed me a box with these pieces when she arrived for the graduation party. I still remember her words: *"We cannot progress if we do not know where we are coming from"*. I was quite confused but when I quizzed, she explained that my mother's family had a long history and life that started in Benin City. She revealed that my mother's great grandfather had worked as a salesman of John Holt, a company that produced and distributed several commodities in the eighteen and nineteen hundreds across West Africa."

Yomba told Chidi the story she was told about how her great grandfather had sojourned to Nigeria in search of greener pastures and landed a job. He met and married a Ghanaian teacher who also lived in Nigeria and they had six children there. Yomba's great grandmother moved back to Ghana with five children, when her husband passed away. However, one of her children, the eldest daughter was already married to a Nigerian, a native of Sapele, and stayed behind with her new family and they never came to Ghana. This Aunty Mildred was her cousin. She was fascinated by the link to Nigeria and had kept in touch with her Aunty and family there. Unfortunately, she had never been able to visit them.

"Ah, so you have Nigerian relatives!" Chidi said gleefully. He said it almost to mean, *you're Nigerian! You're my kinswoman.*

Yomba smiled.

"Strangely, there seems to be a long history of Ghanaians with Nigerian ties. I wonder how it is that I do not have any Ghanaian family members," Chidi said.

"Maybe you are my long-lost cousin. Where did you say you were from, again?" Yomba jested.

"God forbid such a bad thing! You are not my relative."

The thought of any family ties with Yomba made Chidi quite uneasy. An incestuous relationship was not a pleasant thought. It was a conversation he did not want to have and quickly attempted to change the subject. His reaction to the possibility of a family relationship was akin to that of a man who had amorous ambitions towards a young lady, who addresses him respectfully as 'brother'. Whether in the sense of 'Christian brother' or 'big brother', it was the least appreciated expression of respect because that 'title' immediately *zoned* him and prevented any further expression of his appetency.

As if to jostle Chidi back into reality, there was a popping noise heard from Yomba's modest kitchen prompting her to quickly run in.

"Oops!" she exclaimed.

Chidi decided he was better off waiting for her to invite him into the *situation* instead of him intruding. She emerged a few minutes later.

"I was boiling eggs to add to the stew for you and I forgot. The eggs have been on the stove for close to twenty minutes."

Chidi started to laugh and then stopped himself but it was too late; Yomba had already noticed the laughter emerge.

"What is funny? You won't have anything to eat and you're laughing?"

Then he *really* laughed. Yomba was confused. With arms akimbo, she looked sternly at him and asked,

"Chidi, what is funny? Ah!"

Chidi drew closer to her.

"So, you cannot boil simple eggs? A fine girl like you?" And with that, he continued to laugh. Yomba was getting upset with his raucous laughter at her egg mishap.

Chidi settled into a sofa and signalled for her to join him.

"Yomba, I am not hungry. You do not have to look so worried about the eggs. I am not here to judge your culinary skills. Relax! Let's spend this last day we have together well. I beg, forget the eggs."

Yomba smiled. She was not in the least worried about what he thought of her culinary skills, but she was happy to hear him say what he just said. She settled beside him, allowing enough space to make her comfortable as they continued talking about anything and everything. Ever so often, Chidi caught himself wondering how he will cope without being able to look forward to a Sunday afternoon with Yomba. Who said he had to give that up? Accra was just forty-five minutes away from Lagos by air. He could spend every Sunday afternoon with her and return to Lagos on Monday morning.

But my papa no be Dangote,[27] he thought.

"So, when will I see you next?" Yomba asked.

"Well, I want to see you every day, so I don't mind seeing you tomorrow and the day after and the day after and the…"

[27]A line from *Case,* a 2018 single released by Nigerian singer and songwriter, Teni (Teniola Apata)

"That is not what I meant!" Yomba interjected. He knew exactly what she meant. He was just not ready to express what he was feeling about the fact that he will soon not be in the same city with Yomba.

"Yomba, I don't know yet. When are you next coming to Lagos?"

"Maybe in two months. But I get very busy when I am in Lagos, the traffic and hassle of moving from the island to the mainland just keeps me away from any form of social life after I am done with my meetings there."

"Ah! But that is no trouble. I'll pick you up and return you safely to your hotel after we've met. All I want to know is when you're next coming to Lagos so I can look forward to it."

Yomba smiled, knowingly. No words had been said, but she knew where this was going. She was not prepared for it. She did not know how she was going to handle a long-distance relationship and certainly not now when she was so bent on succeeding at her job to please Bose. She was better off just focusing on the task at hand and allowing their friendship to die a natural death.

"Okay, let's set a date. Even if I do not have an official trip to Lagos, let's plan to meet in 4 weeks. Deal?"

Chidi was elated! Yomba was prepared to work towards another meeting. This must be all his mother's prayers at work at the right time. He reached out and hugged her. Quite unexpectedly. She hugged him back. Chidi tried to move away, but he realized Yomba was holding on to him. He closed his eyes and took in the moment. He did not want to spoil it but he wanted more than a hug. It felt perfect and as if she read his thoughts, she snapped up and away from the hug.

"Let's go to the mall," she quipped. "I am hungry. Let's go and get something to eat". She got up off the sofa and headed for her room.

"I'll be back in a few minutes. I have to change."

She dashed off, obviously running away from the mounting emotions that threatened to take over her body. Chidi was momentarily sad, but grateful. It would have taken just another minute and their hug would have evolved into something more – something he knew he was possibly not ready for. It had a way of complicating everything and this time, he did not want to be in a complicated relationship. He was going to wait and watch things unfold naturally: this *one* had to be perfect.

After a few minutes, Yomba walked in, looking casual but sleek. Chidi looked at her and swallowed the lump in his throat. Even after clearing the lump, he could form no words to describe how pretty she looked with all her hair roughly pulled back in a messy ponytail.

"Yomba, I'll miss you when I leave. Let's stay in touch, okay?" Chidi said in a whisper as Yomba drove the car into the street. She tried not to look at him as she focused her attention on the road.

"I'll stay in touch *and*, I'll see you in four weeks, my friend," she replied softly.

Chidi smiled. This was going better than he expected. *My friend?* She had used the personal possessive pronoun, *my*. That was relationship *gold* – he had struck gold with this one. However, it took a minute for him to start doubting her words. What if by that singular comment, she had effectively put him in the friend zone?

No, he thought. This *friend* was different. She had a different tone to it.

He was not just *any* friend. He was a *special friend*. He had a good feeling about this and was not going to allow doubts to steal his joy. He smiled to himself as Yomba drove cautiously to their destination.

****

After grabbing something to eat, they went on to watch a movie at the cinema. The rest of the time was used strolling around the mall, chatting and window shopping. Yomba noticed she was unconsciously hoping the day will not end. But the next day was Monday. *Monday!* The day she so dreaded. Well, that was many hours away. For now, she would enjoy being with Chidi.

Sufficient for today are its troubles, she thought.

After their rendezvous, she drove Chidi back to his sister's and dropped him off at the gate.

"It is too late to go in and say hello," she said.

"You're right. The girls are asleep by now and I'd hate to wake them up."

They both got out of the car and as she leaned in to hug him, he held on to her longer. This time, it was Chidi who did not want to let go of her. Yomba could feel his heart beating against her chest, accompanied by a change in his normal breathing pattern. She gently disengaged and smiled – a very wry smile.

"Good night, Chidi." Yomba said as she sat back in her car.

"Thank you for spending today with me and for every other day, Yomba," Chidi responded as he leaned against the window.

"You're welcome. Accra is better than that your Lagos any day," Yomba jested.

"Better for calm sake and because you live here. That's it. Because you *live* here, Accra will always be better for me. But the day you move, e don finish,[28]" Chidi stated emphatically.

As his words sank in, they both convulsed with laughter. They bid their final goodbyes and Yomba drove off.

As Chidi's figure grew smaller in the distance through her rear-view mirror, she knew she will be counting down to the next time they would meet. She turned on her radio, yearning for a companion on her ride back. There was an entertainment talk programme on, with people arguing about which gender is better than the other. She turned off the radio. She will rather have her thoughts as a companion than have these people bombard her with their arguments – her thoughts and her *memories*. These past few weeks since meeting Chidi had been quite interesting. He was heading back home to Nigeria and she was already missing him. Well, four weeks was not a long way off. Four weeks was twenty-eight whole days. That night, she slept well. She did not wake up to worry about her sales meeting. It was the first time in a long time she had slept through the night. She was happy.

---

[28]Pidgin: It will be over

CHAPTER FIVE

Bose, Mantse, Funmi and Tunde arrived in Accra to Danny's warm smile. Danny was the driver from the car rental company they had booked. He had a piece of paper up that said, *Bose + Family*. When Bose saw it, she heaved a sigh of relief. She did not have a local mobile phone number and had been hoping throughout the flight that the car rental company will not arrive late. The children had so far been well-behaved, but she was pretty sure if they had to wait at the airport for a car to arrive, the story would be different. There was just something about being idle that made Tunde restless and problematic. Funmi was nicely tucked in front of her daddy in a baby pouch. She was getting heavier by the day and Bose was not fond of carrying her in that manner.

"Welcome Madam, this way please."

Danny noticed Bose when she smiled in his direction. That always was a good sign for Danny, who had worked with the car rental company for a good number of years and picked a few hundred passengers from the airport. He had a spot at the arrival hall where he knew none of his arriving passengers will miss him. He always stood at that very same spot. He had learnt the very hard way not to position himself wrongly or get distracted.

He had once missed a passenger because he got distracted by a conversation with a group of drivers. His supervisor had threatened to fire him.

"Because of you, we lost one hundred dollars! The next time that happens, don't bother coming back to this office because you will be fired immediately," he had howled.

That threat was enough to get him mapping strategies at the airport. He had not missed a single passenger since then. Anytime he arrived at the airport, he positioned himself at that very same spot and fixed his gaze on the exit doors. He seldom engaged anyone else around him save the occasional, "Boss, what be your time?[29]" question. A question to which he always had two answers – *a quarter to buy your watch* and the one he spoke out loud, in a curt voice with undertones of *I-am-not-in-the-mood-for-chit-chat-so-please-don't-ask-me-another-question.*

Mantse handed Funmi over to Bose so he could help Danny put the suitcases in the van. They had requested a minivan because they were arriving with seven suitcases, a stroller and two car seats. Mantse had suggested they buy new car seats in Accra instead of travelling with them from

---

[29]Pidgin: Boss, what time is it?

Lagos. Bose disagreed. As he lifted Tunde's car seat from the trolley, he noticed a part of it had chipped, thankfully, it was not broken.

"You see what I was trying to avoid? If this had gotten broken, it would have been a waste of time, energy and money to have travelled with it when we can get one to buy here in Accra," he said, looking at Bose with a *you-don't-listen-to-me* look.

Bose smiled at him instead. She was carrying Funmi and holding on to Tunde's hand who was gradually becoming restless. She was thankful, at least, that the children were calm so far. The chipping of a part of the car seat was the least of her worries. She wanted to get to their new home and begin to figure out this new life in Ghana.

After everything was safely packed into the van and everyone was seated, Danny began to make his exit from the airport parking lot.

"Madam what type of music will you like to listen to please?" Danny inquired just before he exited the terminal.

Bose had never been asked this question by a 'taxi' driver. Not even in Europe where services were perceived to be at their best. Forget New York, she never expected any form of customer service from the taxi drivers there and for as long as she could remember, she had never used a taxi or car rental in Lagos. Before she could afford a car, she rode in a *danfo*[30]. She politely responded to Danny, trying not to sound too surprised.

"Please play anything soft."

Danny chose to play her an Earl Klugh collection he had.

This man must be clairvoyant, Bose thought. Exactly what she needed. Peaceful music to help her relax.

After about 45 minutes of arriving in Accra, they were on their way to their new home. Bose noticed no one was honking incessantly. Maybe because it was a weekend? But there were weekends in Lagos too. What was it that made this city different? Where were all the people, by the way? She did not see the droves crossing at various intersections as she was used to. They arrived in front of a block of flats, *Premier Residences* – which was going to be their new home. *Home.*

***

Mantse was home. He tried not to make Bose feel that he was a tad more comfortable than she was being in Ghana. The truth was, he had longed for an opportunity to be closer to his ageing parents for a while but the discussion of moving the family to Ghana had not featured prominently in their discussions. He was almost afraid to mention it because Bose had hinted to him early in their relationship that she

---

[30]Danfo – minivan used for public transport

had no interest in living anywhere else but in Lagos. He had lost Amy to a similar *move*. He did not want to lose Bose too. Bose had verbalized her aversion to moving to anywhere once. Just once was enough for him.

"Over my dead body will I go and live somewhere else. Lagos is the place to be."

She used the term 'over my dead body' so loosely that Mantse was not sure how to understand it anymore – was it a version of her swearing or was it just for emphasis. He had decided to err on the side of caution and assumed that she was swearing – that the option of living outside Nigeria was indeed very repulsive. Fast forward a few years ahead and here they were about to start a new phase of their lives in Ghana. To Bose, she was an expatriate who had accepted to move to Ghana to build a business but to Mantse, he was home and he had no intentions of going back.

****

Bose started to settle in slowly. With Mantse on sabbatical leave, she did not have to worry too much about care for the children when she was at work. Their father was very capable. They had found a good school for the children in the Cantonments area. Bose was amazed at the school fees initially and wondered if she could have afforded the fees herself. Thankfully, her company was paying – the cost of moving the family and their school fees was built into the compensation package she negotiated.

For Bose, the best thing about living in Ghana was that Mantse's parents were close and could now visit their grandchildren as often as they liked. The worst part? She always felt like a total stranger everywhere she went! All she had to do was start talking and she would be asked: "Are you Nigerian?" Initially, she thought it was just people being nice and she will just smile and respond in the affirmative. Until one day, after a similar question, she asked the lady attendant in the convenience shop she was at why she wanted to know.

"Well," the lady responded, smiling, "you said you want to buy *biro* and only Nigerians call pen, *biro* so I just wanted to confirm."

Bose burst into laughter. So, it was not just her accent, it was also her choice of words. That was a first for her, but it was true. Though quite rare, there was some difference between what she called items and what her Ghanaian colleagues called them. Also, it was how they pronounced words that made it hard for her to understand them and vice versa.

One morning, she got a call from Yomba, who was a Sales Executive in her team.

"Good morning Madam. I hope you're fine. Please, I have a meeting with a client in the opposite block from here so I decided to park and walk. I will be in the office later."

"Okay, that's your work so why are you telling me when it is your work?" she asked surprised.

However, this is what Yomba heard:

"Okay that's your walk, so why are you telling me when it is your walk?"

How sarcastic can this woman be? Yomba thought to herself.

"I was only telling you so you know," she retorted, albeit politely. At this point, Bose was even more confused because she didn't get why Yomba found it necessary to inform her that she was going to perform a duty she *must* perform.

"Yomba, are you at *work*?"

"Yes, madam."

"So, where are you going?"

"I am going to *walk* across the street to a meeting with a prospect."

"Oh, I see! You mean *walk*. No problem. See you later."

She was left gaping in wonder after hanging up the call. She could not understand why Ghanaians pronounced 'work' as 'wek' instead of 'wok'. This was all so confusing for Bose. So, whilst she was hearing "wok", Yomba actually meant it to be something else.

Bose was generally happy in Ghana and settling in quite well. She had her Funmi, Mantse and Tunde and she had a new job that needed her full commitment, but she also had Teddy, who kept checking on her and how she was faring. Life was good. Accra was calm – calm and peaceful but many times, she wondered if she would survive without the hustle of Lagos traffic and the unending need to be in a hurry all the time. She's witnessed how Mantse's transition to Ghana was as smooth as silk and she was willing to try a bit harder. After all, this was her home now – *Ghana* was *home*.

Part Two

"No matter what prison you are in, nobody can imprison the power of your imagination."

Mensa Otabil

CHAPTER SIX

Altimatum Computers Incorporated was a US-based computer firm that was founded by Marjorie and David Miller in Atlanta, Georgia, in the late 1980s. At the time Bose started to interact with them, the founders were no longer directly involved in the business. They had ensured that the business had moved into the hands of Alisa, Chantelle and Marcus, three of their five children who were interested in it. Their two other children – David II and Henry, even though shareholders, had decided to pursue paths in microbiology and fashion respectively.

As such, the Altimatum Computers Inc that was expanding into West Africa was a second-generation company being led by an astute team of Ivy-league-trained business executives who were very sure about their strategic plans and how they were going to implement them. As they deliberated on how to expand into Nigeria and Ghana primarily, their biggest hurdle was deciding on the approach. Should they go in and start their company as a branch of Altimatum USA or as a new business with the same business offering? Should they set up from scratch or would a strategic alliance be a better springboard to start in a market they knew next to nothing about? Why did they even want to expand into Africa?

"Africa has the world's youngest population. It is estimated that about half of Africa's population is under the age of 25 years. This means that there are enormous opportunities for us to sell technology and technology-related solutions in these emerging markets."

Teddy started the justification of the growth plan with these words. He always smiled when he spoke about the opportunities in Africa and particularly, Ghana. Like the founding family, he too was African American but unlike them, he was a third-generation Ghanaian immigrant. His grandparents had moved to the United States as students, met, gotten married and started a family. They later became US citizens and never returned. When Teddy was younger, he remembered being exposed to some Ghanaian culture when his grandparents were alive. But once they passed away before he turned twelve, he had very little memory of that side of his heritage. His father, unfortunately, became so engrossed in making a decent living for his family by working two jobs, that he rarely spent time with them. His mother was *also* African American but five generations of her family had been born and raised in the United States after their forbearers were forcibly removed from their homes in Africa. Shanika, Teddy's mother, though very proud of being black, did not have any real connection to the *motherland* and was therefore unable to teach Teddy and his siblings much about that side of their history. All they knew was what their history lessons taught them and they soon came to realize the truth of the African proverb: *Until the lion tells his side of the story, the tale of the hunt will always glorify the hunter.*

Africa's history as told to them was not, in the least, the full picture. It was a distorted image of a helpless, depraved continent that benefited from dehumanizing experiences like slavery and colonialism. He never understood how colonialism was portrayed as a positive episode in Africa's history. As far as he was concerned, nothing that was said about colonialism could convince him that it was not an outright and deliberate looting of Africa's wealth by Western nations.

Anyway, once the decision had been made to enter two key markets, they started seeking strategic alliances. Their first base was going to be Nigeria, where they will work with independent consultants to gain a better understanding of the market and what needed to be done. Bose had been recommended by a friend of Teddy's, Mark, who had done some business in a few Nigerian cities previously. Mark was a friend of Adaora's and that is how Bose and Mark became friends.

So, Altimatum Computers started with Bose consulting for them and providing leads to companies who may need their expertise. One evening, after a series of email exchanges with Bose, Teddy decided it was possibly a good idea to ask her if she would like the job of Country Manager for their new office in Ghana. Together with the Human Resources department, they had been looking for a suitable candidate for close to six months without success. The issue was that Altimatum had decided to purchase majority shares of an existing Ghanaian company, DataMine Ltd, which had run locally for twelve years but was facing serious financial difficulties. The owners had decided to sell the majority of their shares in the business to allow for a fresh injection of capital to revive the business.

Altimatum had agreed that there will be no staff redundancies. The original shareholders, however, insisted on their retaining significant control of the board and key management positions. They settled on the acquisition deal very quickly; however, Teddy realized they had made a mistake accepting some of the terms associated with the takeover. His rude awakening came with their inability to find a suitable Country Manager. Everyone they headhunted expressed, almost immediately, their unwillingness to work with any company affiliated with DataMine Ltd. Sadly, it was usually after several exchanges that candidates refused to proceed. In one instance, the human resources team had sent an offer, the candidate had accepted but, a week to the resumption date, he had sent a curt email with a 'No thanks' message.

Teddy and a few colleagues had made sure to visit the offices in Accra, met the team and had carried out significant due diligence. Financially, the company was bleeding but operationally, they had a strong team in place with significant experience. The Managing Director was relatively new on the job but was quite pleasant and optimistic that with the new investor, the business would turn around. Everything seemed fine until the pleasant and optimistic Managing Director resigned three months into the acquisition with no notice. They were struggling to find a replacement and it was surprising that all the suitable candidates were reluctant to accept the top job. And, even though the exit of the Managing Director came as welcome news to Altimatum because it allowed them to hire someone, they could trust to implement their strategic plan, they were unprepared for the recruitment nightmare they had to face. The otherwise straight-forward task of finding a Country Manager, (they decided to change the title of the role, in line with their global structure), was proving to be more of a task than they had anticipated.

Teddy decided to take a trip to Ghana to have a meeting with the Human Resources Manager of DataMine. Maybe, if he was in Accra, he will understand how difficult recruiting for the C-suite was. This search for answers led him to Panyin Brown, a Human Resources consultant, who had consulted for DataMine for three years as they tried to restructure the business. DataMine had started experiencing operational challenges in the seventh year of their operations and had to carry out a system-wide redundancy. At that time, they let go of twenty-five of their staff and outsourced most of the administrative functions. Unfortunately, once the restructuring was completed, the Managing Director of the company resigned. The board hired a new one and in six months, the new Managing Director was fired. Since Panyin had worked with them, they had had four Managing Directors, three Sales Directors and no substantive Human Resources Director. Teddy was flabbergasted but there was more to come.

"The board of this company has the owners of the company as directors who sit on the board and control most of its decisions. I believe the main problem is that the board has its nose in every single thing that management wants to do," Panyin said as he peered at Teddy through his thick-lensed spectacles.

"How often are there board meetings?" Teddy asked.

"Once a quarter, but there are emergency meetings called at the will of the majority shareholder and other informal meetings held when required. The Managing Director that resigned just before your company began to engage us, resigned because he was asked to present a monthly report to the board for scrutiny and after haggling with them for three months, he decided he had had enough and resigned. I am not sure there isn't a professional within the technology space in Ghana who does not know about our situation with our board and our high levels of attrition."

"So how is it that you have survived as a consultant for three years?" Teddy interjected.

Panyin smiled whilst taking a sip of his coffee.

"I am 64 years old now. I know how to handle them. Nothing bothers me anymore. I just let them do what they want and at the end of the month, I take my retainer, drive to my farm and rest my mind. The owners are not serious about this business. All they want is money and I am also in for the money. When I'm too tired to work, I will allow my contract with them to end and that will be that."

Teddy was dumbfounded because he had never heard anyone express such nonchalance about anything.

That night, he spent most of the time thinking about how to fix the situation at hand. There was going to be the need for a new set of discussions on how the organisation was going to be run if Altimatum was going to start properly and, subsequently, survive. He needed someone he could trust to lead the change. He realized there was a need for a different direction because, even though they had originally assumed they were acquiring a business with significant equity, they had not anticipated the immense liability of the corporate culture they were going to have to inherit as well. A few days after Teddy returned to his base in Atlanta, he had met several times with the Chief Legal Officer and the Director of Human Resources. He wanted to recruit a Country Manager from outside of Ghana to go in as an expatriate and he had a suitable candidate in mind, Bose, their consultant in Nigeria.

"I do not think hiring a Nigerian Country Manager will be a good idea for a struggling Ghanaian business, Teddy," said Sylvia. "I have done a bit of work in West Africa and the work ethic and approaches in the two countries can be quite different. Besides, there is a subtle, but visible, rivalry between Nigerians and Ghanaians and you do not want to add that to the array of issues we are already dealing with there," Sylvia said.

Sylvia McDery was the Director of Human Resources at Altimatum. She was a middle-aged Jamaican-American woman who joined the company a decade ago in the early days of the exit of the founders. She had become an integral part of the new phase of the company. She started her career as a paralegal in the small town of Akron, Ohio, but moved down south when she "was too fed up with the biting cold of that icy town", as she so regularly told everyone who cared to ask. She then worked with a not-for-profit organisation that supported the resettlement of deported immigrants by providing seed money to them to set up businesses and reintegrate into their societies. The organisation she worked with had partner organisations who worked with the International Organisation for Migration. The partner organisations were in four West African countries – Nigeria, Ghana, Sierra Leone and Liberia. Sylvia worked with a small team that reviewed the business plans that the partner organisations sent in as part of the request for grants.

"I understand your point Sylvia, but do you have any ideas on where we can find a Country Manager because it's been a while now and we don't seem to be getting ahead with this?" Teddy was beginning to get a bit irritated.

Sylvia presented herself as an expert on West Africa and Teddy was quick to remind her that whilst she had worked remotely and visited the region once, he was *from* there.

"Okay, I'll defer to you on this, Teddy. Let's engage her and see if she's interested in moving there. Naturally, the cost of moving her and her family will be borne by the company, which is immaterial at this moment but expensive, I must note. Additionally, there will be a steep learning curve for the cultural issues within the organisation you've already enumerated. We will have to put a plan in place to help her ease in slowly. Give me a few days and let me think about it. In the meantime, please speak with her and then I'll pick up the conversation once she's interested in the role."

"Appreciated. I'll get right to it and let you know how it goes. Michael, thanks for your input as well," Teddy said.

Michael was the Legal Director and, as was characteristic of him, he barely got into any banters that involved Sylvia, and this occasion was no exception. He had sat in the room, simply nodding and responding coyly whenever Teddy looked his way for support and who can blame him? He had been *burnt* once by Sylvia and had decided his mental health was more important than getting her onto his side. Every time he thought about it, he realized maybe, it was time to give up his long-standing grudge and begin to work more cordially with her. She, on the other hand, did not seem to notice that he was constantly avoiding her. She just carried on as her usual self and that annoyed him even more.

Michael and Sylvia joined Altimatum around the same time and had been assigned to the same office buddy to help them settle in. Jeremiah Scotton had worked in the company for a while already before Sylvia and Michael joined and was excited to be the one to help them settle in. Jeremiah's responsibility was to be their first friend and show them around. He took the responsibility very seriously and was known to draw up elaborate plans for newly hired team members which included a lot of informal activities unrelated to work. It was on one such occasion that Michael got his *burning*.

They were walking across the street from their office to a coffee shop Jeremiah swore had the best chocolate chip muffins. As they headed out, Sylvia was telling them a story about her first job and how difficult it had been for her to settle in. She was gleefully explaining why the concept of an office buddy made a huge difference and why she was so happy Altimatum, like so many other progressive companies, had a system like that.

"I'll gladly be your office buddy for as long as you like, Sylvia. It will be my utmost pleasure," said Michael.

"Pleasure? What exactly does pleasure mean, Michael? You started working here three days after I did so how will you be my office buddy? You, like all other men, assume that every woman is distressed and wants to be helped. No, thank you! I will not be the object of your pleasure. I should remind you that I work in human resources and if I, as much as, detect that you are hitting on me again, you will be sorry, *very very* sorry." She stomped off into the coffee shop, leaving Michael perplexed and Jeremiah laughing.

"What did I say? All I did was offer my assistance and I thought it was a joke?" he asked, bewildered at the lecture he just received.

"Well, you must have missed the memo, sir. Women only need male assistance when they ask for it and anything that as much as sounds like you are condescending or diminishing who they are will get you exactly where you are now. In the middle of the street, lost and confused," Jeremiah replied amidst torrents of laughter.

He later tried to explain to Michael what he *felt* Sylvia heard in his remark but for as long as Michael can remember, he did not see anything wrong with his comment. He made a mental note to avoid any semblance of a personal discussion with Sylvia going forward.

Gradually, Michael realized that Sylvia received all information through a special filter – her feminism and her version of it was the strand that had to ensure that everyone was gender-sensitive and inclusive. He was sure there was something about him that Sylvia just did not like and he was determined to stay out of her way. The only snag was, they were both senior managers and had to interact, often. Interestingly, as long as he kept the conversations formal, she was wonderful to work with. Once in a while, Michael will let his guard down and Sylvia will give him a *fix-yourself-before-I-fix-you* kind of look that always reminded him about the first coffee shop incident.

On this occasion, he was simply not in the frame of mind to be on the receiving end of Sylvia's retorts. So, he pretended to be invisible and allow everything that was being discussed to wash over him. After all, if Teddy wanted to hire Bose, he will hire her and there was very little anyone was going to be able to do about it, especially not *madam-know-Africa-well*, Sylvia McDery.

****

A few days later, Teddy had the conversation with Bose. She sounded uninterested initially but had promised to think about it and get back to him. Just as he was heading into the elevator at the end of his typically long day, he took a glance at his phone. He had one new message. It was from Bose and it was just what he was expecting. She was interested in the role. He was excited!

Nevertheless, he will get back to her in the morning; he did not want to sound too excited. If she knew how desperate he was to get her to join the team, that was going to be bad for business. So, he was going to calm down and get back to her in the morning. He slipped his phone into his pocket. He was finally making *progress* – progress in getting Bose to agree to join them. She had not agreed *yet* but at least, she was willing to discuss it now. *That* was progress!

CHAPTER SEVEN

The meeting had been set for 4:00pm on a Friday. A general staff durbar that was going to take more than one hour, yet, they set the meeting time for 4:00pm. *These people!* Yomba exclaimed to herself. She was always so irked when meetings were set for so late in the day. It meant she would not be able to leave the office on time and then, she would have to sit in traffic for up to two hours. *So much for a peaceful Friday evening.* She walked to the conference room with a group of colleagues. Whilst she fidgeted with her phone, she could hear the murmuring around her. No one knew what this meeting was about and the notice they received by email did not say much either. The last time they had such a meeting, it was for the board chair to announce the impending redundancy exercise.

"We sincerely regret that we have to come to this point, but it has become necessary to do this if we are going to be able to survive as a business. Those who are going to leave us will be properly compensated and assisted to get new jobs."

A lady sitting next to Yomba in that meeting had already started sobbing. The room was dead silent. Why they chose to have the meeting on a Friday, to tell them they were going to get fired was something she had since not been able to wrap her mind around. She spent the weekend in a very worrying state of mind. She had worked with the company for four years at the time and this was her first job after university. If she was let go, what will her plan be?

Monday morning, as her colleagues began to arrive, it was obvious many had barely slept all weekend. As much as some tried to hide their frustrations, the tension in the air was palpable. By the end of that day, twenty-five members of staff were let go. Ama Mansa, Yomba's closest office friend, was on the list. She was getting married in a few months and was in school working towards earning a bachelor's degree. She worked in the administration office and had worked as a front desk executive for the last two years since she joined the company. The company had decided to let go of majority of the administrative and support staff whose functions were not core to the business. With that experience, Yomba dreaded meetings that had been called in an impromptu manner and did not share an agenda. More so, she dreaded seeing that the Board Chair was going to be present. She snapped back to reality as someone tapped her.

"Yomba, it has been a while. How are you?" The voice was all too familiar; it was Mr Wink – Kofi, a colleague who always winked at her whenever he had the opportunity.

"Kofi, I'm very well, thanks for asking. How are you too?"

"Could be better. Nothing seems to be working around here. The last event we organized for the marketing team was a huge disaster because that man in the finance office keeps cutting down our budget. He has no idea what it takes to pull off successful events yet, he is quick to cancel out items from *every* budget. He just irks me."

"Well, I understand you. I feel management is just confused sometimes on how to manage the difficulties we find ourselves in. Three weeks ago, they reduced the fuel allowance for the sales team. Yet, the targets have been increased. They expect us to increase our output with less resources. I don't get it!" she exclaimed.

A few minutes later, the room grew silent and the Board Chair, Mr Ekow Sinare, walked in. With him were a lady and three other senior managers including Cornelius, Yomba's Head of Department. The lady was the only 'stranger'. Everyone was eager to hear who she was.

"Good afternoon ladies and gentlemen. I am here to introduce to you, the new Country Manager for DataMine. She has been appointed by the new shareholders, Altimatum, and will lead the company's transformation and expansion efforts going forward. As you know, the Chief Finance Officer, Mr Herdibert Sosu, has been acting as the Country Manager since the exit of the former Managing Director.

The board wishes to thank him for his effort these past six months. Ladies and gentlemen, your new Country Manager is an astute business executive…"

From this point, Yomba was no longer listening. She was fixated on the *lady* being introduced. She was going to be the third CEO since the restructuring started.

Why is she being called Country Manager by the way, Yomba mused.

She looked calm and well put together.

She was younger.

Possibly in her late thirties and she just looked different.

"She is Mrs Bose Mensah," Mr Sinare's voice gave her the last piece in the puzzle.

She was Nigerian. The first Nigerian to work in their company.

She was different.

Yomba hoped and silently prayed that she will be different in a good way.

****

Monday morning. It was Bose's first day at work. Her driver picked her up at 7:00 am and it took forty-five minutes to get to the office – from her apartment in Cantonments to the office in East Legon. She had spent the time in the car observing the behaviour of drivers in traffic. She wondered how it was that this rush hour traffic seemed so *sane*. She was not going to ask any 'JJC'[31] questions. Her driver seemed like a nice man, but she was not sure what he would think of her should she begin to bombard him with questions. When she arrived in the office, the security guard at the entrance greeted her and waved them in. She smiled and waved back.

"Good morning madam. I am Erastus and I am your personal assistant. Unfortunately, I was not around on Friday so we could not meet."

"Good morning Erastus. Nice to meet you."

He walked with her into the building and up a short flight of stairs to her office. She had been shown around on Friday and had made a mental note of where her office was located. She did not remember the stairs. She did not like climbing stairs because she typically wore high heels and her biggest phobia was basophobia. She had once fallen in front of a group of boys whilst in primary school. She could not remember what made her fall, but could remember how loud the laughter of the boys was.

---

[31] JJC – acronym for Johnny Just Come. This is a term used to describe a newcomer or a stranger who knows little about their environment.

After her brief meeting with Erastus, she sat in her office just looking around. She had come along with a small box of items she felt she needed – a framed picture of her family, a small potted plant, a desk planner and her mug that said "Rock Star Mum", which Mantse had bought for her one weekend as they lazily strolled in the mall with the children. She had been worrying about how Tunde and Funmi will settle into school in Ghana and Mantse was trying to reassure her. They walked past a home décor shop and Mantse spotted a selection of mugs. They went in and he bought her that particular mug.

"You will be fine, my dear," he assured, hugging her from the side.

"Thank you," Bose replied, returning his hug.

It was a good reassurance for her and she had decided to bring it with her to work so she could have it as a reminder whenever she felt inadequate.

Her mind drifted to the staff meeting that was held the week before. She had arrived at 3:00pm to meet the Board Chair and some senior management of DataMine – Mr Ekow Sinare – a pleasant elderly man. He was a retired public servant and looked like he had lived a full life. After a brief interaction led by the board chair, Bose and the other senior managers headed off to the staff durbar. But that meeting had ended faster than she could say "Jack Robinson". Not that she had anything to compare to, really, but she felt the room was too quiet and the people too unresponsive to the announcement of a new country manager. She had expected an avalanche of questions and had prepared, no, *worried* and then prepared, for several possible responses throughout the night. When Mr Sinare had asked if anyone had a question, a young man blurted out from the back of the room:

"Madam, are you married?" The room erupted in a burst of thunderous laughter.

"Yes, I am," Bose responded with a smile.

When the laughter subsided, Mr Sinare ended the meeting with a curt reply.

"Well, if you don't have questions, we will call it a day. Bose, welcome to the team. We wish you well."

With that, the meeting was over as quickly as it had started.

Bose felt the whole conversation was a bit detached and rushed. Her expectation of what a meeting of this nature was supposed to be was quite different from what had happened. Maybe, her expectations were too high?

Snap out of it girl! There is work to be done, she said to herself.

Now, she was sitting in her new office wondering where to start from. *Erastus!* She will get assistance from him. She wondered how, of all the names available under the sun, her assistant would go by that name. Why *Erastus*? Panyin Brown had mentioned to her on Friday that she had a personal assistant who will help her settle in. Before meeting him, she assumed he was possibly an older man and was surprised to meet a young man in his late twenties, bespectacled and sharp looking – with a name that sounded like he was in his seventies.

Erastus had been with the company for three years and had recently been moved from the Human Resources team into the Country Manager's office. She had never had a personal assistant whilst she managed her own business. This was a pleasant novelty for her. She just did not like the ring to his name, *Erastus*, because it sounded like a character in Greek mythology.

"How did you get the name, Erastus?" She asked when he had walked into her office to discuss her itinerary for the day. Erastus smiled gently. It was not the first time he had been asked. He had a prepared answer.

"My parents were both academics and at the time I was born, my mum was studying towards her PhD in Classics and Philosophy. She had always liked the sound of the name. She wanted to call me Zeus originally, but my father disagreed and they arrived at a compromise – Erastus. My father calls me Nana Yaw, which is also what most of my friends call me, but my official name is Erastus."

Bose smiled at him. That was a lot of information as an answer to a simple question.

"I see. So, what do you want me to call you? Nana Yaw or Erastus?"

"Please call me Erastus. It means lovely."

"Sure thing! Nice to meet you, Lovely," Bose extended her hand to shake him.

"The pleasure is mine, madam."

"You can call me Bose."

"Yes, madam Bose."

"Just Bose."

"Yes madam, ermmm. Yes Bose."

"It will be hard to call you Bose, but I will try."

"Thank you, Erastus. Let's meet in an hour. I will need you to help me settle in and we have loads of work to do."

"Yes, madam... Yes Bose," Erastus responded and left her office to his, which was an adjoining room to hers.

Bose's office was nicely designed but she expected she will make some changes to how it looked. There was a chunky sofa that she did not like. *What an ugly looking piece of furniture.* It looked like an invitation to guests to relax and never leave. She began to make a list of what she needed in her office when her thoughts were interrupted by a light tap on her door. Erastus emerged.

"Hi Bose, there is a standing management meeting at 11 am. Should I cancel it for this week?"

"No, please don't," Bose responded. "Let's have the meeting."

Erastus proceeded to give her a brief of how the meetings were conducted. He had a bulky folder of minutes and his laptop bearing semblance to a court clerk with a docket of pending cases.

"Our meetings are long," Erastus intimated, stretching the word 'long' for emphasis. "This is what happens – we start the meeting by going over the previous minutes and the floor is open for inputs to be made: input they could have made during the days before the meeting if only they had read their emails. But no one reads emails here. So, I make all the corrections at the meeting. It has gotten better though; Maribel helps me a lot."

"Who is Maribel?" Bose inquired.

"Oh sorry, I assumed you had met her. Maribel is the head of IT. She helps me with the editing right after the meetings. One of the only senior managers who reads emails without having to be prompted."

"Great!" Bose said. "Please continue your narration."

"Madam, sorry, Bose. Some of the managers always come up with reasons why they have not completed assigned tasks. Some come to the meetings late and others have been known not to show up at all with no reason. I wish you will simply cancel these meetings."

Bose smiled. Erastus sounded like he was really flustered. She was no fan of long meetings, especially those that were long and produced no results. She *just* could not stand them.

"Mr. Sosu chairs the meetings, right?"

"Yes, he does."

"What is that look on your face, Erastus?" Bose probed.

"Hmm, Madam. Mr Sosu has been unable to enforce anything. He allows everyone to say what they want and do as they please. There was once a full-blown argument in the meeting between the Marketing Manager and the Procurement Manager about a delayed payment to a vendor. The two gentlemen were almost involved in a fisticuff. It was Maribel who finally managed to end the brawl."

Bose listened to Erastus in amazement. She had no real experience with large management meetings. Her meetings, in the past, had been quite intimate and fast-paced. She decided to observe the first meeting and then make a decision on how she would like the meetings to run going forward.

"Erastus, we have 45 minutes to the meeting. I'll be right back." She headed out of her office to find Herdibert.

Herdibert Sosu was a chartered accountant and a pleasant middle-aged man. He had worked with DataMine for five years after a long career in the civil service. He had moved around Ghana quite a lot working as an auditor. He had joined DataMine after he refused the fourth transfer in three years. It was rumoured that his persistent transfers were due to an altercation he had had with the Chief Director at the ministry he worked for.

Bose got to his office. She gently tapped on his door and walked in. He had his back to the door, something she found pretty odd. People usually faced the door in their offices so they could see whoever walked in. Herdibert had his back to the door. His desk was spotless and paperless. Bose's first impression of him - *possibly-doesn't-do-any-work*.

Weird.

"Hello, Mr Sosu," Bose greeted, prompting Herdibert to turn in what could be mistaken as a twirl by a young ballerina, the only difference being that the character was a man in his early fifties wearing a tie that seemed a bit too tight for his neck.

"Hello Bose. To what do I owe the honour of this visit? Please take a seat," Herdibert offered.

Bose sat down and quickly looked around.

He is either very organized or does absolutely no work.

"Mr Sosu, I'll really appreciate it if you could chair the next three management meetings whilst I observe. I have been told you were managing the team in the absence of a Country Manager, and I'll like you to work with me over the next month as I settle here."

Herdibert was surprised by her request. Most people will jump at the opportunity to show who is boss the moment they had a chance. This was a first.

"Sure, that is no problem at all. I will assist you."

"Thank you, Mr Sosu," Bose said as she extended her hand to shake Herdibert.

"You're welcome, Madam."

She smiled and walked out of Herdibert's office. He seemed like a nice man – a nice man with a really clean office. She was sure she will like working with him.

****

The management meeting started and ended well. Strangely, only one individual arrived late and she explained that she had to attend to an emergency in her office before leaving for the meeting. Herdibert took updates from all the functional heads. Bose was listening but not listening. She was paying attention to the personalities in the room. There were eight people in the room: Maribel Gyimah from IT and Digital Solutions; Cornelius Amanor from Marketing and Sales; Kofi Manu in charge of Procurement and Supply Chain; Herdibert, the Chief Finance Officer; Sophia Ahmed, the Human Resources manager; and Solomon Grant, the Corporate Affairs Manager. Erastus was present to take minutes.

Bose occasionally glanced around the room as each of them presented their reports. Herdibert rarely interrupted and only asked questions when they were done. Cornelius, in his sales update, said: "I hope the following month's revenue will be better" and this is what arrested Bose's attention.

Hope? Was that what he was banking an increase in revenue on? Ah well, let's see how this goes.

Then there was Sophia giving the recap on a situation she was resolving relating to disciplinary action. Two staff members were the subject of an ongoing investigation that involved a customer who had reported that they physically assaulted her. The customer claimed she was ruffled up when she complained about a service failure and mentioned two of their staff as being the ones who pushed her out of the office. Sophia, in concluding her report stated: "We *hope* to complete the investigation later next week and present the report to management. Hopefully this will not occur in the future."

Hope! Again!

"Herdibert, I'll like to make a few comments if you don't mind."

"Sure, go ahead."

"Sophia, can you confirm to us that we will get the final report at our next meeting?"

"Yes madam," she offered a laconic reply.

"That's great. So, it is not that you hope to, but that you *will* complete this investigation and we *will* have the report during the next meeting?"

Sophia looked at Bose with obvious confusion.

"I'm not sure if you've said anything different from what I already said, Madam," Sophia said with a slight tint of anger behind her words.

"Just a slight difference. You used the word *hope* and I am using the word *will*. I don't want to *hope* you will complete this task; I want to know with all certainty that you *will*."

Erastus giggled; Bose shot him a stern look.

The room was dead silent.

"Thanks Bose. Sophia, we will look forward to your report at the next meeting," Herdibert stated, coming to the rescue.

He then proceeded to take final comments from everyone, gave his closing remarks and then closed the meeting. Bose noticed everyone was still seated even though the meeting was over. Herdibert rose and began to walk towards the exit.

"Thank you very much, Mr Sosu. I appreciate your support."

"You're welcome. There are a few things I have to discuss with you offline, so I will check on your availability later today and possibly swing by your office."

"No problem at all. I'm sure aside lunch and my going to catch up with Erastus, I have a very light day."

"Sure, we will talk later then," Herdibert responded whilst briskly walking to his office.

"Erastus, please remind me to meet with Mr Sosu before I leave today. We need to catch up in my office after lunch."

"Yes, madam... sorry, Yes Bose."

Bose walked to her office, with Erastus at her heels. Herdibert was several steps ahead and she could not help but notice Herdibert's quick gait. She smiled to herself.

This is going to be one interesting ride.

CHAPTER EIGHT

It had been just nine months since Bose joined the team at DataMine. The change in leadership had become evident, at least to Yomba. The Sales and Marketing team used to meet twice a month, now, they met every Monday morning and Bose was in attendance at *every single meeting*. The first meeting went well. It was about three months after she joined. She interacted with all twelve members of Cornelius' team and got to know them. She listened to them as they gave updates on their sales leads and the constraints that needed resolving.

Yomba liked Bose as a person when she first joined the team. She liked that she was pleasant and open-minded. Then the meetings became more frequent and held earlier in the day: Monday at 9:00am, and Bose was never late. She also did not tolerate lateness. Yomba always ensured she was early after she witnessed Kofi being called out for walking in late during one of their meetings. Kofi, alias Mr Wink – a nickname only Yomba knew – had walked in ten minutes late to the departmental meeting. He quickly slipped into a seat closest to the entrance to not distract anyone; however, Bose noticed.

"Welcome and thank you for joining us. Can you please tell us why you are late?"

Kofi smiled, being his ever-relaxed self.

"Thank you, Madam. I had a car problem. I apologize."

"Car problem? I see. I am sure if you had to be at a visa interview at 9am, you would probably arrive at the gate of the embassy a clear two hours to the appointment." She paused for a few seconds, as if to get a response from Kofi. Then she continued. "I do not expect that with the level of performance of this team, anyone will take these meetings lightly. I do not tolerate lateness at my meetings. If I can get here on time, you have no excuse. I hope this is clear with everyone."

There was no response.

Kofi was silent. He was not sure what had just happened. The truth was he did *not* have any car trouble. He had simply overslept and left home a bit later than normal. He felt Bose was overreacting and was embarrassing him.

"I hope this is clear?" Bose repeated, obviously expecting an answer.

"Yes madam," Erastus said, acting as a spokesperson for the group.

Bose looked at him sternly for a second and proceeded with the meeting.

Cornelius looked like he wanted to explode. His meeting had not only been hijacked by Bose, but now, she was embarrassing one of his star team members.

Yomba wished he had spoken up but he did not. He simply looked at Bose and made it obvious he was upset. The rest of the meeting was a blur; however, Yomba vowed she was never going to be late to any of Bose's meetings. *And,* that is how her Sunday night to Monday morning panic attacks started.

Bose required that each member of the sales team gave an update on their pipeline deals. She had hiked up the weekly call plan target and expected them to do twice the number of sales calls than they did before she arrived. Cornelius had tried to talk her out of it, indicating that the market was tough and that customers were opting for cheaper internet solutions for their businesses and homes. DataMine had also not fully built the infrastructure to be able to reach customers nationwide. There was stiff competition from the telecom companies and DataMine continued to see a decline in its market share. Cornelius had this conversation with her in the presence of the rest of the team. Bose was not having any of it: she pushed ahead with her plan on increasing the targets of the team.

After that meeting, Cornelius resigned. He submitted a resignation letter to Sophia and stormed out of the office. Yomba could see him drive out of the building from her desk. He had not said anything to the team before leaving but they knew what was happening. Cornelius rarely got upset. But he had exhibited his dissatisfaction and despair openly at every opportunity since Bose became the *de facto* head of department. The next morning, they got an email from Solomon, the Head of Corporate affairs. Management was announcing the resignation of Cornelius Amanor, the Head of Sales and Marketing. In the interim, Maribel Gyimah from IT would be the acting in his stead.

Maribel had worked closely with Cornelius whilst he was around. They were into the business of selling internet solutions and the unit that developed what they sold was Maribel's department. She frequently sat in on their meetings to get customer feedback and a sense of what the market needed. She had worked in DataMine longer than any other senior manager and was considered a suitable candidate for the Country Manager role when it became vacant. When Bose was introduced, rumour had it that she had threatened to resign. She was on leave for two weeks into Bose's first month and that fuelled the rumours even more. When she returned, however, there was no evidence of dissatisfaction. She was her regular self and worked well with Bose as she did with everyone else.

Yomba had given a replacement for Cornelius very little thought. She assumed Bose will act in his place whilst they looked for a replacement. She was still reading the email from Corporate Affairs when she got a message notification on her phone and looked at the screen. It was a message from Chidi. They messaged each other multiple times during the day and then spoke in the evening on her way home. Because Nigerian time was one hour ahead of Ghana, Chidi was usually home when she was on her way. He was a good traffic companion and they typically spoke until she arrived at her apartment. Then, she will go off the line to grab something to eat, settle in, have a quick shower and they were back on the phone again. Averagely, they spent about ninety minutes on the phone every evening, catching up with what happened at work, what happened in their respective cities and then they spent some of the time laughing and 'gisting' as Chidi called it.

"How now?"

"I dey. How be?"

"By God's grace but, I have missed you."

Yomba rarely responded to his attempts at endearment.

"Charlie, I have to gist you. Your Naija sister just forced my boss to resign."

"No be one mama and papa born us. I beg she is not my sister[32]," he responded.

---

[32]Pidgin: We do not have the same father and mother. We are not siblings

"I hear you. We will talk after work."

"No wahala."

"Later."

Yomba looked at her watch. It was 9:45am. She had to finish a couple of proposals and then head off to a client meeting at 11:00am. Cornelius was gone and she had a new boss. Tuesday to Monday was not too many days and she needed to work hard at her targets so she had a good report to present.

****

Bose was working late with Erastus because they were preparing for a board meeting. Just as she was winding down, Sophia tapped on her door. It was late and almost everyone had left the office. She was not expecting anyone to tap on her door.

"Hello Bose, I was just leaving but I saw the lights in your office still on, so I decided to pop in and give you some information."

"Hello Sophia, sure, please come in. Kindly take a seat."

Sophia sat down.

"Bose, Cornelius turned in a resignation earlier today. He stated personal reasons and try as I could, he did not want to disclose the reasons for his sudden resignation."

"He resigned? Wow!" Bose exclaimed. Her heart began to race, and her mouth felt dry.

"I'm very surprised he will do that. I hope it is not because of what happened this morning at the team meeting."

Sophia was silent. Bose got the message.

"He resigned because we disagreed on the target set for the team? I expected that he will come to me after the meeting to try and get his message across. I meant to call him after lunch but got carried away trying to finish these board reports. Wow!"

Bose was standing now. Pacing slightly. Erastus walked in.

"Bose, do you need something? I thought I heard you call me."

"No, I didn't call you, Erastus," Bose responded as calmly as she could.

"Are you done with the final edit?"

"Almost madam."

"Okay."

Erastus had not heard his name. He was simply being his nosy self. He heard Bose's raised voice and decided he wanted to know what the issue was. He had allowed Sophia into the office just a few seconds ago thus, whatever it was that Bose was raising her voice about had to be important and serious. He hoped it was not something that could not be resolved. At least, Bose was doing a good job at keeping everything afloat. He was sure she could fix whatever it was that Sophia had told her. For now, he had to focus on completing the report for Bose. The board meeting was in two weeks and she was required to send in her report to the Board Secretary so the board papers could be sent to the board members.

"Sophia, thanks for letting me know. Do you advise I try and call him?"

"You could try but I already tried to reach him several times today and his phone is off. Maybe we need to give him some time and try again in a few days."

"If his phone is off, then there's no point in us trying to reach him. He does not want to be reached. We need a replacement for him as soon as possible. Let's discuss first thing tomorrow morning: Solomon, Herdibert, you and me. I'll send a message to the rest of them for an 8:30am meeting."

"That's fine. I'll leave now. Have a good evening Bose."

"Thanks, Sophia. Wishing you same."

Sophia was not sure if what she was feeling was surprise or awe. Bose had sounded 'affected' by Cornelius' resignation but almost immediately, she was ready to replace him. The shift was just so sudden. Almost like saying, *good riddance to bad rubbish*. As she drove home, she kept thinking about Bose's reaction. She needed to figure out what their plan will be for that role, especially since their revenue figures needed to be consistent to ensure profitability. They will figure it out tomorrow. Tomorrow will take care of itself.

Cornelius' resignation was a big blow to Bose. She had run-ins with colleagues in the past and publicly disagreed with colleagues, even as the CEO of her own company, but she had never had someone resign because they did not agree with her approach or perspective. To make matters worse, Cornelius had resigned the very same day after they had their disagreement. She felt it was nothing personal and that he was simply protecting his territory. But to *resign?* That was extreme. What a time for her to lose a key member of her team! She was not sure if she was upset that he left or sad that he had left over such a *flimsy* reason. She knew she had been hard on him and his team but it was all in the interest of the business. She had no ulterior motives. She was not a bad person and when she accepted to move to Ghana with her family, she knew it was not going to be a funfair. But she had not been prepared, mentally or emotionally, for what just happened. The board papers could wait. She closed her laptop, grabbed her handbag and headed for the door.

She would usually ask Erastus to tell her driver to bring the car upfront. This time, she had not done that requiring Erastus to break into a sprint to find the driver who was possibly asleep in the driver's lounge at the back of the building. Bose had to wait for a few minutes but Clement, her driver, was soon there.

"Madam sorry. I didn't know you were ready to leave."

"It's okay, Clement."

She got into her car and curtly waved at Erastus who was huffing and puffing after his sprint.

He knew how Bose disliked waiting for the driver when she was ready to leave. So, he had told her to give him the heads up a few minutes to when she was ready to leave so he could call the driver. That was their normal routine now. But today was not normal. Bose was not in a good mood. He will have to wait to find out what the issue was. He sat back in a chair, trying to catch his breath before heading in to complete the document and email it off to Bose before leaving.

His phone rang. It was Bose.

"Hello, Bose…Yes, please… Yes please. 8:30am… Okay. Yes, I've noted the names. You mentioned Solomon, Sophia and Herdibert. Would you want me at the meeting? … Yes, Bose. I will do so immediately. Good night."

He had one more task for the evening and it seemed it was more urgent than the report he was editing. He began to type the email and his phone rang again.

"Hello, Bose... yes, please. I will do that. Thank you."

She wanted him to send out the email but she also wanted him to call the three individuals and let them know there was a meeting for early the next day.

"I don't want someone to say they didn't see the email and so they are not aware," she had said.

Erastus did as Bose had instructed. He sent the email and then called each of them. It felt like performing a task twice but he was not going to take any chances of getting into trouble with Bose. He could simply have called each of the three individuals and be done with it. But she had asked him to send out emails and *then* call. Unfortunately, he did not know what the agenda for the meeting was and did not want to call Bose back. Solomon and Herdibert wanted to know but he had no suitable response for them. They both stated they will call Bose directly.

Well, that's above my paygrade, Erastus thought.

It was almost 8:00pm and he was now possibly the only person left in the office.

He kept at the report and completed it, then did a quick walk-through to Bose's office to make sure she had shut down everything. She had. He always checked and she always turned off everything that had to be turned off. *This lady is perfect.* He smiled and headed for the exit. Without traffic, it took him forty-five minutes to get home and then, he typically spent another hour talking to his dad and mum before heading off to bed. His parents had both retired and he was living with them. He had two other siblings who were younger but had left home. One was married and living with her husband and the other, his younger brother, was working in Obuasi, a city about five hours drive from Accra.

Erastus was thankful to his parents that he did not have to pay rent. But in the same vein, he hated the look his female friends gave him whenever the subject of living arrangements came up. One of his closest lady friends once said to him:

"Nana Yaw, I think you are still living with your folks because you do not want to commit to a relationship. You are being selfish".

Erastus' reasons were purely economic. He had been working for three years and because he was not paying any bills, had been able to save enough money to buy a small second-hand car. Several of his mates who were paying rent were still taking public transport. He, however, was concerned about the commitment part. The truth was, he could never take a friend of the opposite sex to his home. The one time he invited a female friend to his home, his mother immediately began to quiz him.

"Ma, she is my friend. We just met. She is not even my girlfriend yet and you're asking if she is my fiancé?"

"So why did you bring her to meet us then? She's a lovely girl by the way. When I was your age, I had already settled down with your mum and you were on your way."

"Yes, you got her pregnant, Daddy. You were compelled to marry her."

"No! I was going to marry her anyway; you just came along sooner than we planned and we decided to get married earlier than we had expected."

Professor Kofi Larbi was a tall lanky sexagenarian. He walked to where his wife stood and put his arm around her.

"Your mum has always been my biggest achievement, Nana Yaw. I pray you find your own love sometime soon and start a family."

"Yes Pops. I have heard you for the one-hundredth time and for the one-hundredth time, I am not ready to settle down."

That is how the conversation always ended and it seemed his parents were not letting down on the 'get-married-soon agenda'.

He tried to avoid it and that meant preventing his female friends from visiting him. Coupled with the amount of work he had to deal with – being the personal assistant to a chief executive, he barely had a social life. He had vowed to stay for five years before moving out of his parents' house. That way, he would have saved enough money to rent a nice apartment close to the business district. No amount of *marriage pressure* was going to make him change his plans.

His drive home was quiet. No traffic. No conversation. Just his thoughts and wondering what had made Bose's mood switch so quickly. He would find out soon enough.

****

The ride home for Bose seemed too long even though it was her regular distance. She wanted to get home and let out all the different emotions she was feeling. Was it anger or frustration? Was it sadness or guilt? She did not quite know.

"Clement, please turn off the music." Clement obliged.

She whispered a "thank you" under her breath. Too faint to be heard by Clement. It did not matter because Clement knew there was something wrong with his madam.

Bose closed her eyes and the first image that came to her was of Sophia's demeanour as she conveyed the news of Cornelius' resignation. There was something in her voice and her tone that communicated: "You pushed him to leave". It was her tone that was making her feel what she was feeling.

However, she couldn't even decipher if her feelings were out of anger or guilt? *Guilt.* She felt guilty. And oh! She was also very confused because she had not seen it coming. Why would anyone resign because they disagreed with their boss? Was it cultural or was it because he had other plans?

She arrived at her apartment. Got out of the car and said good night to Clement. She walked as if in a trance – visibly exhausted and emotionally drained. She let herself into the apartment. Mantse was sitting at the dining table typing away on his laptop. He raised his head and flashed her his best smile. Almost immediately, he noticed there was something wrong. Bose usually got home tired, but that never prevented her from walking over and hugging him. This evening was different. She walked in and sat down on the closest sofa to the door. She reclined her head and within seconds, Mantse could hear what he knew had to be sobs. Bose was crying. He walked over to her.

"Bose, what is wrong?"

She continued to cry. Mantse held one of her hands and slightly lifted her drooping head by touching her chin.

"Babes, what is wrong? Talk to me. Did something happen at work? Did you get any bad news from Lagos? Is Mama okay?"

The pace of questioning from Mantse was in congruence with the intensity of the flow of tears from Bose. It was almost as if Mantse was making the situation worse by asking questions. He noticed he was not making any headway. He put his arm around her and allowed her to cry. After what seemed like forever, Bose's tears began to subside like flood waters recede after heavy rains in the city of Accra, *soon* to be forgotten.

"One of my colleagues resigned today and I think it is my fault. We disagreed in the morning and right after that, he put in his resignation. All I did was try to get him to agree to some stretch targets. He disagreed with me and I pushed back. He resigned, Mantse! Resigned!"

She said the word 'resigned' like someone will say the word "died". As in, *he died… he just fell and died…* with the *can-you-imagine-that* tone. Mantse was not sure of what to say or how to say it. A resignation was normal. *Why was is she crying? Bose crying?*

"Bose, I don't think your colleague resigned because of you. Maybe, he just wanted to move on."

"Move on?" Bose's voice was slightly raised. She stood up.

"How can he want to move on in the middle of a difficult situation and why is it that it was just today he decided to move on. After we disagreed? I don't think that is it Mantse. This guy just left because of me. How am I going to…?"

Mantse did not allow her to say anything more. He got up and pulled her to his arms.

"Madam, it's okay for one day. Calm down. I am sure by the time you wake up tomorrow morning, you would have figured out what to do with this situation. For now, you've had enough. You're beginning to turn this on me." He chuckled a bit on the last statement.

He knew Bose well; he had been at the receiving end of some of the transferred frustration from work, quite a number of times. He knew the symptoms too well. She would raise her voice, try to explain and before long, the frustration would have been turned on him. He was not going to allow that to happen today. He was becoming an expert at deflecting the negative energy and getting her to relax.

"Okay. I hear you. But I am hungry and tired."

"There's food in the kitchen. I left you some of the dinner the children and I had. Let's go; we can eat in the kitchen."

"We? You never chop finish?[33]"

"I will help you. Let's go."

---

[33]Pidgin: Haven't you already eaten?

That made Bose laugh. Mantse was always 'helping' her with her meals. It did not matter how much he had eaten before she got home, Mantse always took a bite out of her meal.

She ate her dinner and they got ready for bed. Just before she closed her eyes, Bose turned into Mantse's arms.

"Thank you… for everything," she said, almost inaudibly.

"Ermm, I am not accepting verbal gratitude tonight Mrs. Mensah. I am only accepting…"

Bose was laughing now.

"Oga, I beg, I don taya[34]. Let me sleep for some few hours; I'll wake you up, don't worry."

"Ermm! I hear you but I might as well just forget it for tonight. I always wake up disappointed after such promises," he added looking forlorn.

"Oh Mantse, today will be different; I promise."

She turned, her back towards him and pulled his arm around her.

"Okay, I hear you though…" His words were interrupted by Bose's heavy breathing which was characteristic of a sleeping Bose. It took her seconds to fall deeply asleep. She was exhausted. Not just physically, but emotionally too.

---

[34]Pidgin: Boss, I am tired

Tomorrow, they will figure out the rest of the task at hand but till then...

As he hugged her tightly, he knew she was going to sleep till morning. Not tonight. Tonight, she did not have a headache, which he knew the *perfect* cure for, tonight, she was sad. That was different. He will allow her to sleep and hope she wakes up some time before morning. It was always different at dawn. Maybe at dawn.

****

Bose spent the next few days after Cornelius' resignation preparing to meet her board. It was a crucial board meeting because it was a half-year review and Bose was also inching to her first year anniversary of being with the company. Her brief from Teddy had been quite clear when she was starting – reorganize the team and put the company on a trajectory for growth and expansion, and that was what she had focused on. She had highlighted the key initiatives in each key unit and provided project timelines for what she was doing towards the transformation and how much progress had been made. On the day of the board meeting, she was very confident about the results she was going to share and was positive. It was her second meeting with the board, they would be happy with the results of the first half of the year. They had not achieved all the set targets across the operation but, she and her team were on the right path towards achieving, at least, seventy per cent of the goals set. The meeting was set for 10:00am and the venue was the conference room adjoining Bose's office. Thankfully, all seven board members arrived on time and the company secretary called the meeting to order at 10:05am.

The company secretary – Audrey Banson, a lovely petite lady who had worked with this board for five years, passed around the board documents to enable members to read the minutes of the previous meeting. Even though copies of the minutes were always shared electronically to board members, Audrey knew too well that some board members never got around to reading theirs. She was never wrong with her assumption. Thus, she always came prepared with hard copies to ensure the smooth running of the day's agenda. However, her efforts were thwarted by the fact that, not only did they not read the minutes, but they also hardly read the presentations and reports sent ahead. This meant everything was going to be discussed from scratch at the meeting, thereby dragging the meeting longer than it should actually be. Aside from the seven board members and board Secretary, Herdibert and Maribel had joined Bose as management team members to present reports. Bose would present her report first, followed by Herdibert and Maribel in that order.

After a few corrections to the previous minutes, it was time for Bose to present her report. She proceeded to present the key issues and areas of impact. She was just on the second of fifteen slides when she was interrupted by Professor Gordon, one of the board members.

"Madam Country Manager, how many slides do you have?"

Bose's neck stiffened at that question. She had sent this report two weeks ago to the company secretary and she had assumed the board members had made time to peruse the documents.

"Sir, there are fifteen slides in all. I am reporting on the top-level items and my colleagues will provide details in their reports. My slides are only highlighting the report. I sent the actual report ahead to Audrey so I assumed you've had a look at it?"

"Audrey sent an email with this report?" he questioned turning to look in Audrey's direction.

"Audrey, you know that I hardly check my emails. You should have called me to inform me you had sent a document. Bose, I have not read the documents that were sent but I think fifteen slides is too long for us to sit here and listen to. Can you cut it down?"

He had not allowed Audrey to respond and Bose was too surprised at the ease with which he declared that he was not in the habit of checking his emails.

Bose was tempted to ask, w*ho, in this day and age, does not check their emails and needs to be prompted to do so?* But she caught herself and allowed Audrey, who was visibly uncomfortable with the development, to speak.

"Prof, I called you twice last week but your phone was off. I, therefore, assumed you must have been out of town. I sent you a text but got no response. We send the board papers, at least, two weeks ahead of the meeting so may I please advise that members endeavour to check their emails when there is an upcoming board meeting?" Audrey added firmly.

"You're right Audrey. I was out of town in a village in the Western Region – very close to where Herdibert used to work. The network was very bad there so I didn't bother to put my phone on. I will…"

"Prof, please offline with Audrey on that. We will have to proceed otherwise we may never be able to complete today's meeting. We have to be done by 1pm and there are two other report presentations for us," interrupted Mr. Sinare, the board chair. It was his attempt to rescue the situation before the Prof took them totally off tangent.

Professor Gordon was a sixty-five-year-old university professor who taught history and classics at one of Ghana's leading universities. He had worked on a project for DataMine as a member of the consultancy firm he had set up with three other lecturers. After the project had ended, the erstwhile management of DataMine had asked him to join the board and he had been on the board for a decade. He was the longest-serving board member and also the most likely to make a meeting run forever, with his constant interruptions.

Bose continued with her presentation. She was on her seventh slide – talking the meeting through the performance updates and showing what progress the company had made on all the key performance indicators when she was interrupted again. This time, not by Professor Gordon.

"Bose, are you trying to tell us that even though you have only achieved sixty-five per cent of your revenue targets, you are still doing well? How and when did sixty-five per cent of a target become recognized as good performance? I mean if you are sixty-five per cent on target, you should be telling us how you intend to close the gap instead of trying to make it look like the team is performing well..."

Bose had to interrupt.

"Mr. Wengam, I would get to that point shortly. If you could refer to the report I sent *ahead of this meeting*," Bose stressed, "I did mention that the performance, though below expectation, still showed strong indications of growth when compared to the previous year. I will allow Maribel to present more of those details when it is her turn and in order not to preempt her, I will limit myself to the year to date performance as well as highlights of the year over year growth. I hope that is fine with the board?"

"I think what Spencer (referring to Mr. Wengam) is trying to say is that we cannot accept a sixty-five per cent performance with the description of being good. You stated somewhere that you were positive about the results..."

you should not be positive about such results!" Mr. Sinare interjected.

"To make matters worse, the remedial measures are nowhere on this slide. Hence, I'm finding it very difficult to see where we are heading with the presentation," Spencer reiterated, glad that there was someone in the meeting who agreed with his position.

Bose was trying to remain calm.

Will these people just allow me to finish? Gosh! She thought to herself.

Spencer continued, "Bose, do you realize that you were brought to lead a turnaround situation? I don't see the energy that is required to do so in this report. I will even say you are wasting our time with this presentation if it doesn't tell us how you intend to improve the fortunes of this business before the end of this year."

"Mr. Wengam, I think you will need to allow me to finish my presentation before you draw those conclusions," Bose responded curtly.

"Okay. But we do not have all day." Spencer said, whilst slightly reclining in his seat and folded his arms across his chest. Bose got the message: *Let's see what you have there and mind you, we don't have time to waste.*

Spencer Wengam was a shareholder of the business. He had co-founded it and was one of three majority shareholders who had sold a percentage of their shares to Altimatum Inc. Bose had been happy to note that one of the founders was on the board but what she did not expect was that Spencer was going to be a thorn in her flesh. From that point on, Bose raced through her slides. She was livid but trying to keep her composure. She ended her presentation and as soon as she took her seat, the board chairperson inquired from the board if there were any issues members would like to ask the Country Manager or should they proceed with the next presentation? They had no further questions and the other reports were presented.

The meeting progressed in the same fashion: Professor Gordon asking questions not linked to the reports, Spencer making snide remarks and Mr. Sinare trying to mediate. The four other members rarely spoke and if they did, it was in agreement to whatever Spencer was saying. By the end of the meeting, Bose was exhausted and upset. The meeting ended five hours after it had started and two hours after the scheduled end time.

There was an invitation to lunch; however, Bose declined and indicated she would rather stay in the office and finish up on some of the requests from the board so that she could submit the report and recommendations for approval. Maribel and Herdibert, however, went ahead with the board members. Bose had hoped they will all decline and was astonished that they did not. Lunch with this bunch after the type of meeting they just had? That felt like such an oddity, but she looked in the direction of Maribel and Herdibert and realized that declining was *the* oddity. She was now the odd one out yet, she was fine with that. She had no intentions of sitting at lunch with Spencer and Professor Gordon – she had had enough of them for one lifetime. Sadly, this was going to be her life every quarter as long as she stayed with the company. Before she could leave, Audrey pulled her aside.

"You will be fine. Don't give too much attention to them. Just focus on what has to be done."

"Thank you, Audrey. I appreciate this," Bose said with a wryly smile. It was the first time anyone had said anything encouraging to her in the company. She was not sure how to react.

As she got into her office, all she wanted to do was shut down her laptop and go home. She will give it a few minutes, allow the board members to leave the premises and then make a dash for it. She picked up her desk phone.

"Erastus, can you please have Clement ready for me in fifteen minutes?"

It was a few minutes after 3pm and Bose had never left at this time of the day. Something was wrong. *Again!*

CHAPTER NINE

It had been six weeks since Cornelius resigned and Yomba was beginning to feel that, in spite of his flaws, he had been a better boss than her new 'interim-boss', Maribel. Yomba had always liked Maribel from afar – she liked her for her *shoe-sense*. She had taken notice of the fact that Maribel never repeated a pair of shoes during the week and, in some cases, over several weeks. Yomba always wondered how many pairs she had. Maybe, now that she was working with her, she would ask her. *Maybe?* Heck no! How was that conversation going to start? She had played it out in her mind a couple of times.

Hello Maribel, nice shoes.

Thank you, Yomba.

Do you have like a thousand pairs of shoes?

... and how does that impact on your sales performance, Yomba. I think you should be focusing more on how to achieve your targets than paying attention to my shoes so much. I'm sure if you put just a bit

more effort into your work, you will not have to come up with so many excuses when asked questions.

Her mind would always run wild with how the conversation would go and it always gave her the shivers.

Yomba had been on a steady ascent with her work and she had begun to get more comfortable with how she reported her progress and her challenges during the team meetings. She had no reason to be terrified of Maribel, but she was. Why did she miss Cornelius though? Even though Maribel was a pleasant person, she came across as a tyrannical leader who never listened to the team; she also did not seem to understand their frustrations. She hardly offered to assist the team on sales calls and would demand of them, tight deadlines on projects. She also seemed totally at sea when there were technical sales issues to resolve and that made Yomba quite frustrated. For instance, Kwame, one of her team members, had encountered a challenge with a prospective customer who had a previous bad experience with the company and whom the company was trying to win back. Everyone expected that Maribel will offer to go with Kwame to see the client. She did not. Kwame, after waiting for a few weeks and reporting on the same issue, was compelled to ask out of frustration:

"Madam, I was hoping you'd go with me to see Mr. Akabutu. I'm sure since you're the boss, he may feel more comfortable talking to you and will calm down a bit on the issue. When Mr. Cornelius was here, that is what he used to do to help us with difficult customers."

"But I am not Cornelius," Maribel said sternly

"And I do not babysit adults at work. If you cannot do your job, we should be having a conversation on how to put you on a performance improvement plan instead of you talking about how Cornelius did his job and how you expect me to do mine."

Kwame had no response. The room went dead silent. That was the end of the discussion on the matter and Kwame neither reported on the account again, nor brought it up for discussion at any of their meetings.

In another instance, she had used a word they had never heard to describe the performance of one of their colleagues.

"This level of performance is sheer criminal," she had said. *Criminal?* That was a word associated with jail time.

Then there was that one time she had asked them to submit their sales report on a daily basis by 4:00pm and, even though they had explained to her that 4:00pm was unrealistic because they were out of the office most days until about 5:00pm, she insisted. Yomba had been the one to speak up at that meeting. One of those times she hoped she had kept silent.

"Maribel, is it okay if we sent it to you much later in the evening?"

Maribel did not respond for a few seconds and then looked at Yomba.

"*4pm*, Yomba. 4pm is when I want to receive your reports. Thanks for asking."

Cornelius had not insisted on strict delivery timelines for the submission of reports. In fact, the convention was that when he demanded for something by 'close of business', it actually meant 'by midnight' of the day in question. Maribel was not having any of that and obviously, the team was struggling with adjusting to her style of leadership. Interestingly however, after their first three team meetings, Bose stopped attending their meetings. The rumor mill had it that Bose had opted not to attend because she was confident in Maribel's approach. What they did not know was that Maribel had requested that Bose allow her to manage her team directly without any interference. She wanted time to work with the team and develop a system that worked. She believed that having the Country Manager attending their sales meetings was putting pressure on the team and their performance would be affected in the long term. Bose agreed with her and offered to support her whenever she needed assistance.

****

A few days had passed since the board meeting and Bose was still processing the experience. Her first meeting with the board had been so pleasant and cordial, she wondered what had changed. She had completed the required documents from the board meeting and sent them off to Audrey. After her email was delivered, she got a call from Audrey and after the initial pleasantries, Audrey began to speak to the real reason she had called.

"I was going to suggest that you call Professor Gordon and let him know you have submitted the updates to me. Then possibly call Spencer as well, just so you…" Bose did not allow her to finish.

"I do not think I should be the one calling them, is that not what the company secretary does?" she asked, trying so hard to hold back her building rage.

"Indeed, but I noticed you may have to do a bit more to get into their good books and ensure that the next meeting is better than the last one we had. I've worked with this board for quite a while, I know how they think," Audrey said.

"Oooh okaaay… that's fine. Thanks, Audrey." She almost added, *for your unwanted assistance.*

Then she remembered she was a professional working as the Country Manager of an organization; she was not having a conversation with Adaora or even Mantse.

The phone call came to a polite end. Bose was beginning to appreciate Audrey's willingness to help her 'fit in'. But she did not want to fit in. She did not want to kowtow to the whims of these men. She was beginning to get very irritated with the fact that she had to massage their egos to get on well with them. Why could she not just work and let her work speak for her as it always did when she was running her own business? She had experience working with egotistical men trying to tell her what she could or could not say or how she should go about getting a big contract, but she had never had to work *for* them or think of them beyond a particular transaction. In this instance, she *reported* to them and they had their noses and their fingers and their heads and their whole beings in the business. *What a board!* Just thinking about them was making her heart race. She was getting stressed, already.

Calm down Bose. Calm down. She sang to herself.

"Babe, can you talk?"

A text message from Adaora. Bose called her immediately.

"O girl! How now? Country manager or should I say *kantri* manager?"

Adaora made it a point to always tease Bose with the Ghanaian accent that she found totally hilarious. Bose was trying to adjust and sometimes mentioned words in a more Ghanaian way, something that made Adaora so amused.

"Adaora, can you imagine what just happened? I was just called by our board secretary to call two of our board members and to tell them I have sent my report so I can warm my way into their hearts. See me see trouble o. Did I come to work or I came to make people feel good?"

Adaora was laughing.

"The same board members who gave you a tough time the last time? Well, it's not a bad idea... You may want to take her advice."

"Ah Adaora! Do I look like someone who wants to be friends with them? I came here to do my job, I will do it well and when I'm done, no be commot I go kuku commot for here?[35]"

"Yes now, but before you leave, you should try and get along with them. I don't know how it is like to report to a difficult board, but I will tell you how I have managed my uncles in this our family business — make them feel important, win them to your side and then do what you have to do. They won't notice."

"Adaora! You? I want to laugh."

"Yes o....na me[36]. My uncles are very important to my mother and I realized that all the animosity was affecting her

---

[35] Pidgin — translated as "I will just leave when I'm done here"

[36] Pidgin: Yes, it's me.

more than it was affecting the business. So, I hatched a plan. I call them often. I ask for their advice. I pretend to do some of the things they say, but I don't and at the end of the day, we are all happy."

"Eiii! Adaora, nicely done. Okay o…I hear you. I will try."

They proceeded to spend the next few minutes catching up with all the news from Lagos. Adaora updated Bose on all she had missed out on so far. Which companies were securing which contracts and what industries were thriving under whose leadership. She did not leave out the juicy details of who just had a flamboyant five-star wedding or birthday party and the fact that the eldest daughter of a senator had been reported to have had her sixteenth birthday party on board a yacht. There had been a party to celebrate the headmaster of the secondary school they both attended and from the pictures Bose had seen, she knew she had missed out on quite a lot of fun with old school mates. But here she was in Accra, trying to massage the egos of two grown men.

"Adaora, you have to come to Ghana for Christmas. The children miss their Aunty Adaora. Come and relax in my nice Ghana."

"No wahala[37], biko[38]! I will try and get away from my *wek* and then come and spend some time with you in your *kantri*."

---

[37] Pidgin: No problem

[38] Ibo word for please

Her attempts always made Bose laugh and Bose's laughter was contagious. They were both laughing.

"We will talk again, thank you for calling."

"No wahala… I will call you next week."

"Bye!"

"Bye!"

Bose loved speaking to her friend, Adaora – she was morphing right before her eyes. Adaora used to be this hard-headed businesswoman from Onitsha, who was constantly trying to outwit her uncles and did not give a hoot what they thought. That same person was advising her to engage her nemeses. *People change, indeed.*

Bose checked her phone's address book and found Spencer's number. She dialed it. The phone rang a couple of times before it was answered.

"Hello, this is Mr. Wengam's phone."

"Hello, may I please speak to Mr. Wengam. I am Bose, calling from DataMine," she responded.

"Mr. Wengam is in a meeting please. I am Sika and I work in his office. Would you like me to pass on a message for you?"

"Yes, kindly tell him I called and he can return my call when he's…"

"He has just walked in," Sika interrupted. "Please hold, let me see if he will like to speak to you now."

The line went silent for a few seconds.

"Madam Bose, good afternoon."

"Good afternoon Spencer. I hope all is well."

"Yes, I am well, thank you for asking. Is there an emergency at DataMine? You have never called me before and…"

"No, no emergency. I am just calling to let you know that I have submitted the additional documents requested after the board meeting. I was wondering if you've received them and would like to discuss."

"Oh, okay. Thank you. I have received them but I am yet to read. I will do so before the week runs out and if I have questions, we can meet to discuss."

"Thank you, Spencer, enjoy the rest of your day."

"Thank you, Madam Bose," and with that, Spencer hanged up before she could say *you're welcome*.

Hmm! Nawa o…was it the same Spencer?

A few days ago, he was charging at her at the meeting like a wounded lion. Maybe, this was a different Spencer. He sounded so calm. *Almost* friendly. But friendly, or friends was not a zone she wanted Spencer in. Calm was good enough – anything that was not the same as how he was at the board meeting was acceptable. She could live with *calm*.

She thought to call Audrey. But she felt she would rather finish the discussion with Spencer and then give her a full update. She was still processing her thoughts and her just-ended encounter with Spencer when her phone beeped with a text notification. It was from Audrey and the message read: You called Spencer? Thank you for listening.

Wow, word travels fast in this place!

Was it Sika who told Audrey or Spencer did himself? There was no way for her to find out without asking Audrey. But it was not urgent, even though she was very curious. She decided she was not going to pursue it. She was feeling good about herself having called Spencer. She just hoped this was not going to go south sometime soon. For some reason, she simply did not trust this new Spencer and his calm demeanor.

****

The sales team was beginning to form well and were no longer 'missing' Cornelius. Maribel was happy to report to management that the reports were coming in on time and everyone had settled into a routine – *her* routine. She, however, did not add that the sales meetings were less interactive. No one wanted to question her authority or make suggestions: they simply presented their reports in a very orderly structured manner, just like she liked them. *Structured.* They had nicknamed her – *Bell Woman.* Kwame had started it. Maribel usually sent an email at the beginning of the week to the whole team with all the things she expected them to do and their respective timelines. She also always had a statement in her emails:

Kindly endeavour to submit all tasks on or before the stipulated deadline.

After reading one of such emails, Kwame, unable to contain himself, blurted out in the office.

"This woman sounds like she's our house mistress and we are being reminded about rising bell." Everyone burst into laughter.

"Maybe, she is the bell woman. Always sending us reminders. Let's get her a bell – Bell Woman. It even sounds like her name – Maribel – Bell – Bell Woman!" Kwame was laughing and feeling like a human thesaurus.

As time went on, Maribel began to feel the pressure of managing two key roles but she had set her mind on something else. She wanted to be the Country Manager of DataMine. She had always wanted to be. She perceived her current situation as a phase – a phase for her to prove herself and finally get into the role that she had *worked* for for the last few years. But did she really want to be Country Manager? Maybe, maybe not. For now, she was just going to focus on her dual role. The sales team seemed to be finally getting into the flow and she was hoping in another few weeks, the company would have made a decision about a replacement for Cornelius so she could return to her real job, the job of becoming a Country Manager. She had left the management of the marketing side of the business to the Marketing Manager – Koomson, whom she believed could handle the key issues.

As much as she would not want to admit, she was impressed with the productivity of the team and she was confident they will end the year well, in relation to their targets. The only snag was, she knew they did not like her but she did not care. She always remembered her mentor's words as he quoted Machiavelli:

"It is better to be feared than to be loved if you cannot be both".

****

After being on sabbatical leave for close to a year, Mantse was getting tired of having so much time on his hands. He liked being around the children, but it felt like he was missing out on life by being at home. His mother's impression of his sabbatical leave had been borderline hilarious though it *did* give him some food for thought. Did he want to take an extra year off or was it better to get back to work now. Interestingly, none of the comments from family or friends mattered to him as much as the concern expressed by his mother. She simply did not understand how he had a job in Nigeria and was now in Ghana, not working and had been at this 'leave' for almost a year.

"What kind of leave is that? If you have been sacked, tell us you did something and you were sacked. Don't tell us cock and bull stories, my friend!"

The way she said the last phrase "my friend" was not in an endearing manner.

"Sacked? Oh Mama, I have not been sacked. As a university lecturer, I can take a year off from work to pursue other interests, rest and research. My university still pays me but I am not there physically."

"Okay o, I hear."

She had heard him but she did not believe him, at least, according to what his sister told him a few weeks later.

"Your mother thinks you are jobless and living off your wife. You have to explain to her well what sabbatical leave is."

"But I have done that and she still doesn't understand," Mantse replied, obviously frustrated with the news.

"Well, she said if you're on leave, you can still get another job that will send you out of the house every day. To her, a responsible man is one who goes to work every day – a sign that he is taking good care of his family," Naa said rolling her eyes.

"Hmm, but who told her I am not taking care of my family?"

"She said her friend who lives near you guys told her that Bose leaves early in the morning and returns late and all you do is take the children to school and pick them up. Big brother, you're officially a house husband!" Naa said with an irritating guffaw and she was so lucky she swerved her brother's friendly knock that almost landed on her head.

Mantse was not *too* concerned at first but began to get concerned at the description of 'house husband' when it was first used by his sister, Naa. *So, what if he was a house husband though? How was that anyone's business?* He thought to himself. It was quite normal in Canada to see a father being the main care giver to his child, but he did realize he lived in Ghana now and that concept was seen as alien.

It did not help much that Bose also laughed when he narrated the discussion he had with his mother.

"She thinks you've been fired? That's so funny!"

She was sitting on the floor with her legs on the sofa beside him. She had the interesting habit of using the sofa as a foot-rest instead of putting her legs on the centre table like everyone else would do. She had always done that and Mantse had always found it cute.

"Any way, we need to think about how we will manage with the children once I get back to work. Should we get a nanny who will help out?" Mantse was almost soliloquizing because he could notice Bose nodding off.

"Hmm, I'm not sure. Let's wait and see what your teaching load will be and then we can make a decision."

"Yeah, that can be a plan. But what about if I take the job in the University of Cape Coast? We will need to make a decision as soon as possible."

"Sir, I am tired. Please let's discuss this tomorrow. I promise."

Mantse smiled. He knew when his wife was avoiding a difficult conversation and he also knew when she was plainly tired. Today, she was tired.

"No *problemo*, but you're not falling asleep on that floor, madam. Please get up and go to the bedroom now. I don't want to have to wake you up and you'll be all cranky with me," Mantse stated emphatically.

"I am just resting a bit; I am not sleeping. I have to wake up to work on a report," Bose replied knowing very well that Mantse was right with this one.

"Please I have heard that story before. You can 'rest a bit' in the bedroom."

"Oh Mantse, why are you worrying me? Trust me, I will get up in about an hour to work."

"Hmm, okay. But if you don't wake up, I will leave you here until morning, and don't come complaining to me that your neck or back hurts from sleeping on the floor," he warned.

Bose got up and dived into the three-seater sofa across from where Mantse was sitting.

"I will not complain to you, this sofa is comfortable," she smiled, propped up a throw-pillow and closed her eyes.

Mantse knew he was fighting a lost battle. They had this conversation many evenings. Bose will fall asleep on the floor in the living room or in the sofa. She will pretend not to be sleeping but he will return after several hours and she will be asleep, curled up like an orphaned child.

He would wake her up and she will walk to the bedroom and continue sleeping. Yet, the next day, she will insist she was just 'resting' for a while and will wake up to complete a report of some sort.

Mantse knew the routine now and this time he was not having it.

"Bose, no. Please get up now and let's go to the bedroom. If you want to work in the night, you can work there. But I am not coming back to wake you up. Let's go to the bedroom now."

"Ooooh ah! Okay, okay. Let's go."

She walked off angrily.

Why was he so difficult to convince? Can't a woman rest in a sofa again? Does that have to be a big deal? Why are men so dramatic? Gosh!

It was as if Mantse could read her thoughts, because his *dramatic* took a different turn.

"Madam, you are wearing your office clothes. Don't you want to take a bath before you sleep?"

"Ah Mantse! I said I am just resting. I will wake up later to work. When I wake up, I will take a bath." At this point, Bose was no longer sleepy. She was wide awake and upset.

"Just take your bath now. Or do you want me to bath you?" Mantse asked, almost in stitches. He was having a good laugh, internally though, at her expense.

She was sitting up on the bed and looking at Mantse, peeved to the core.

"You are very lucky that I like you. You are very lucky," Bose quipped.

"You are very lucky that I love you, Bose. Very lucky," Mantse responded at his sarcastic best.

Bose got out of her clothes and walked into the bathroom, smiling to herself. Truth be told, she was a handful and Mantse was managing well. As she started to take her bath, she began to reflect on the conversation they had just had.

House husband.

That would not be a bad idea at all, at least, until the children were a bit older. But he was a university professor. Did he want to be a *stay-at-home* dad?

Time will tell, she thought to herself as the water cascaded downwards with her back turned to the shower.

****

Yomba and her colleagues arrived at work one Monday morning to the news that their colleague, Kwame, was unwell and on admission at the hospital. He had sent a text message to a colleague in the early hours of the morning and an image of him being given intravenous medication.

Kwame was one of the most eclectic team members and so when he was unwell, it was like having a missing piece of a puzzle.

"Kwame is unwell today. Hopefully, he will be back during the week. Yomba, I'll forward to you his last report so you can follow up on the urgent pending issues," Maribel had said in a very dismissive manner after their team meeting.

"Yes please," Yomba responded.

The day went by in a breeze for Yomba. Covering for Kwame, in addition to ensuring that her tasks were completed, was more than Yomba wanted to grapple with on a Monday. As the day drew to a close, she began to feel resentful that Maribel had given her so much extra work. It was 7:00pm and she was not yet done with everything. Her colleagues began to file out of the office and the enormity of her workload dawned on her. To add to her woes, her back hurt, her eyes ached and her tummy churned. The number of proposals that needed to be sent out to prospects was mainly what was weighing heavily on her. How was it that Kwame had so many 'pending - proposal' items in his report? Eight out of his fifteen items were about proposals and Maribel wanted her to draft those proposals before she left the office.

Kwame. She had made a mental note to call him at some point during the day. It was evening now and she had not done so.

Well, she thought to herself, *I better do it now.*

She picked up her phone and put in the letter 'K' in the search box. She had simply saved his number as 'K Colleague'. They called him 'Kay' around the office instead of Kwame. This was because there were three other Kwames in the company. The phone rang for a while before a feeble sounding Kwame could be heard on the other end of the line.

"Yomba, what's up?"

"Hey, Kay, how are you doing?"

"Charlie, not good o. I think I have food poisoning; I ate something over the weekend that messed me up."

"Wow! Then it's really bad. You sound awful."

"Hmm... I think everything in my stomach, along with my intestines, has come out by one of two ways from my body."

"Sorry o. So, when do you think you'd be out of the hospital?"

"I think tomorrow. I feel better than I did when I got here late last night."

"Cool. Then there's no need to visit you. I'll call you in the morning."

"Sure. How is Bell Woman? Did she say anything about me?"

"Not really, she just mentioned you were unwell and made me follow up with some of the things in your report. I am working on the proposals you have to write."

"Proposals? Which proposals?" Kwame quizzed, accompanied with a laugh.

"What is funny, Kay?"

"I just put that in my report so she won't ask too many questions about them at the meeting." He continued to laugh, albeit quite weakly.

"You! What nonsense! Do you know how hard I've worked today? Ah Kwame," Yomba paused, in a bid to control her anger. "You're not serious." Kwame's laughter was ringing in her ear and even though she felt 'wasted', she was relieved to hear him laugh.

"I'll get back at you, just get well and get back to the office. We've missed you already," Yomba replied as she found the humour in the situation.

"Don't worry, I will sort you out when I get back. I will help you with one of your PowerPoint presentations, okay?"

Yomba could not help laughing. Kwame was terrible at creating PowerPoint presentations and he was offering her, the office PowerPoint *guru*, assistance in that area? After speaking to Kwame, she knew it was time to leave the office. There was no point working on his phantom proposals. She will call Chidi on her drive home and though he will have a good laugh at her expense, it will surely help her relax.

She shut down everything and turned off the lights. She was the last person to leave in her office. She looked across the floor and noticed that Maribel's office had lights – *Bell Woman* was still working. She decided to go over and say goodnight. A gentle tap on the glass wall was enough to catch Maribel's attention. She looked up from her computer and saw Yomba.

"Hey Yomba. You're still here?"

"I'm on my way out. Just wanted to say good night."

"Oh thanks. Good night."

"Yomba," Maribel called as she turned to leave. "Did you call Kwame today? I have been meaning to, but I've been so busy."

"Yes, I just called him."

"Oh, that's great. How is he doing?"

"He was not his usual self though but we spoke for a while."

"That's good to know. I will call him in the morning. I don't want to bother him now."

"I am even sure he will be sleeping by now."

"That's fine. Good night."

"Good night."

Yomba continued on her way as her heels clicked clacked on the tiled floor of their office building.

Maribel was nicer outside of meetings. Wow.

She will get into her car and do what she does as a routine most evenings: she will call Chidi and they will discuss how their day went as she drives home. It helped her relax and, on days that she was very tired, prevented her from falling asleep behind the wheel. She looked forward to her drive home now and there was something else she was looking forward to – December and Christmas.

Chidi will spend two weeks in Ghana with his family. Who was she kidding? She was looking forward to his visit more than his family. He was coming to Ghana primarily to spend time with her. The last time she saw him was almost three months ago when she had gone to Lagos for a client meeting with Maribel and another colleague. This time, her fear of flying was not as bad and she felt more relaxed taking the trip. It was understandable because all she was thinking about was getting to Lagos, finishing with her meetings and then meeting Chidi. He had volunteered to meet her at the location of her last meeting and take her to her hotel. He was on time. They did not go to her hotel. They went to the Ikeja Mall, sat on the balcony and just talked and laughed for what seemed like forever. They parted with the promise that they will meet in December. It was in December they had first met almost two years ago, and she was so looking forward to seeing him again.

****

Mantse and Bose made a decision about how they were going to figure out Mantse's next move. He was going back to teach but will accept a teaching job at a University in Accra instead. It had taken a lot of consideration and the willingness to accept a lower compensation package but Mantse felt it was important for him to be available in Accra to support Bose. She was getting more and more frustrated at work and arriving home looking more and more drained. He was seeing a shadow of the bubbly, energetic woman he had married. She explained to him the many run-ins she was having with her board and, worse of all, the inability of their US-based partners to get the board and shareholders to realign the business. She had been hired by Altimatum Inc. and Teddy, along with the senior management team responsible for their global expansion, had been very clear to her on what they expected her to do. After a year, things were simply not going the way they expected.

Mantse knew it was not a good time to be gone from his family for five days out of the week. This was not the time to leave Bose with the responsibility of thinking about children and their home all by herself. Secretly, he felt guilty for encouraging her to move away from her home to Ghana and to take up the new role Teddy had so nicely sold to her. He, therefore, felt duty bound to support her to succeed and if she was not succeeding, be with her when she failed. He never told Bose what he was feeling but when he announced to her that he was not moving to the University of Cape Coast, her spontaneous embrace of him was all the evidence he needed to confirm he made the right choice.

"I never wanted you to go there but I didn't want to discourage you. I mean, Cape Coast is not that far from here but the thought that I'll come home in the evenings and you won't be here ... who will wake me up and force me to go and sleep in the bedroom?" she said jokingly.

"Exactly! I don't want you to spend five nights sleeping on the sofa. By the end of one semester, you'd have become a full tenant of the living room. How will I then get you back into the bedroom?" They both laughed. Bose stopped to look at Mantse.

"Mantse, thank you. Thank you for everything."

"You're welcome darling... you're always welcome."

****

Kwame did not recover. A week after getting sick, he was diagnosed with an aggressive form of sepsis. His body was unable to fight the infection and he passed on. Maribel was the first to learn of Kwame's death. She had made it to the hospital to visit him after he was unable to return to work in the first week due to the new diagnosis. She had met his mother and two sisters and had exchanged numbers with his youngest sister, Lucy, who happened to have attended the same secondary school as she had. For some strange reason, the moment the phone rang and she saw who the caller was, she started forming a cold sweat on her brow.

"Aunty Maribel," Lucy said, amidst sobs. "Kwame didn't make it. He died early this morning. The doctors said the infection was too strong. My mother said I should call you," she concluded.

Maribel was quiet for a while. She was not sure what to say and how to process what she was feeling.

"Lucy, thank you for calling. I'm so sorry for your loss. I will call you back, okay?" This was all she could manage before hanging up the call. She could have said more to console the young girl but, she had to end the call quickly because she did not want to break down. Kwame was not her favorite person but he was a member of her team. She picked up her desk phone and called Sophia.

"Hello Sophia, Kwame didn't make it. His sister just called me... yes. I'll pass on her number... okay. Yes... an email to staff will be great before they hear it elsewhere. Thank you."

CHAPTER TEN

The days that followed the death of Kwame proved to be very difficult for Yomba. Kwame was one of her closest colleagues. Everyone in the company had been so saddened by his sudden departure but Yomba was possibly the worst hit. She had been in touch with him frequently and they kept joking about his phantom list of pending proposals. Until two days before he passed away, he was texting her regularly. Then he went silent. She had tried to reach him, but her messages were undelivered and unanswered. Then she got an email from the Human Resources department.

"We regret to announce the sudden passing of our friend and colleague, Kwame Asenso. He was a member of the..."

She could not read beyond that point. Her vision was blurred and the tears had gathered like clouds in readiness for a heavy down pour.

Her colleagues were talking all around her and Akosua was crying. Yomba was numb. She had not imagined that this will happen. She had not expected it and, therefore, had not prepared her mind for it. Is anyone ever prepared for the loss of a colleague and friend? Thankfully, she had no meetings scheduled for that day, so she quietly rose, took her phone and went to the restroom. She needed a moment alone with her thoughts. No sooner had she entered the restroom than her tears began to flow. She cried for what seemed like forever and then sent Chidi a text.

"My colleague didn't make it. He passed away." Her tears dripping on the phone.

Almost immediately, her phone rang. It was Chidi. She picked the call.

"Yomba. I'm so sorry."

She continued to cry. No words were exchanged. Chidi was silent. All that could be heard was the high-pitched sound of silence – the silence between two individuals who have an absolute knowing that the person on the other end of the line was listening. Simply listening. That was all that Yomba needed at this point.

"Chidi, I have to go back to my office. I am in the restroom... okay, I will. No, I don't have any meetings today... okay. I will call you when I get home. Yes, I will take a taxi."

Yomba left the restroom with the intention of packing up and leaving the office. It was going to be very hard for her to go through the day in the state that she was in. Chidi had suggested that she leave her car and use a taxi to get home.

"Call me when you get home," he had said. "But don't drive."

She had started packing up when Maribel showed up in their office. It was an open-plan office with several workstations. A few of her colleagues were huddled together talking about Kwame. Akosua was no longer crying but she was not working either. Everyone was just literally unable to process what they had just been hit with.

"Hello guys, I know you're all sad at the moment. Kwame's death is a big blow to everyone, but we have to keep working. You have a report due later today. Let's get back to work," Maribel said, walked out of the room and headed towards her office.

Yomba was not sure what had just happened. Did she hear properly or did she imagine what Maribel just said?

Let's get back to work?

Yomba continued to pack up. She did not announce her departure, she just left the office. Hailed a taxi from outside their premises and headed home. Her ride home was quiet. Thankfully, this taxi driver was not one of the regular chatterbox drivers who provided unsolicited advice on life, love, politics and everything in between. He was quiet.

Yomba arrived at her apartment and her phone began to ring. It was Maribel. She decided not to pick. She was not ready to have a conversation with anyone just yet. She allowed the phone to ring. Maribel tried to reach her twice again. Yomba did not pick. She got a text message from Akosua right after:

Maribel has asked that we all meet her at 3pm today to discuss the plan for the rest of the week. Where are you?

3:00pm was forty-five minutes away. There was no way she was going to make it. And even if she could make it, she did not want to be in a meeting today. Not with Maribel, not with anyone. Yomba sent a text to the only person she was willing to speak to at the moment.

"Chidi, I'm home now."

"Okay, rest a bit and I'll call you in about two hours. I need to finish up a report."

"Okay. Catch you later."

"Be safe."

Yomba walked into her bedroom, lay down and slept. When she opened her eyes, it was 7:00pm and she had been asleep since about 2:00pm. She looked at her phone. She had six missed calls – two from Chidi, one from Akosua and three from Maribel. She decided she would call Maribel back first. Maybe, she was simply worried about her whereabouts seeing that she had not told anyone she was heading home. She dialed Maribel's number and after a few rings, Maribel was on the line.

"Hello Yomba."

"Hello Maribel."

"Yomba, where are you? I have been trying to reach you because we had an emergency meeting and I needed updates on a particular account you are working on."

"Sorry I just had to leave the office. I was not feeling very well. I needed to be alone."

"Yomba if you were unwell, you should have told me. We really needed the information from you to process an invoice. By the way, do you realize that it is unacceptable to simply leave the office?"

Yomba was not sure whether to be sad or angry. She was not sure how to process the emotions that were rising in her heart. But she knew they were negative and she needed to keep her mouth from saying what was in her heart. So, she kept silent and let Maribel talk.

"Yomba, can you hear me? You cannot just *leave* the office. Do you want me to have human resources send you a query?"

Still silent.

"I will give you time to think about what happened today and we can talk tomorrow morning. Please come to my office when you get to work."

"Yes Maribel," she responded feebly.

Maribel hung up. Yomba stared at her phone. Kwame passed away. Maribel is upset that she left the office to process her feelings? Maribel expects her to work as if nothing happened? Maribel is upset that she left the office?

This cannot be real!

Next, she called Chidi. Who better than her friend to neutralize the effect of her insensitive boss?

"Hey. Did you sleep well?"

Chidi spent the next fifteen minutes on the phone with Yomba. They talked about everything and he let her cry a bit more. By the time they were done, Yomba was exhausted. Tomorrow, she will meet with Maribel and face up to what *tomorrow* had in store for her.

****

It had been a while since Bose last spoke to Teddy. Apart from a few emails they had exchanged in the early days of her taking up her role at DataMine, Teddy has become quite distant. *Distant* not in terms of geography, but in terms of relationship. He was not the Teddy who cajoled her to take up the role and was definitely not the Teddy who had 'protected' her from the iron fist of Sylvia. And so, an email from him indicating he was heading to Ghana in the next 24 hours came as a surprise to her. His email was more of a text message.

Hey Bose, I'll be in Accra in about 24 hours. I'm getting on a plane now. I'll like to catch up with you. I'll call you when I arrive and we can agree on a time to meet. Cheers. Teddy

Bose read his email a couple of times and wondered whether it was worth responding. She wanted to ask him a number of questions but maybe 24 hours was not too long to wait. She simply responded:

Hey Teddy, nice to know. See you soon and safe journey.

She hit send.

Then, she began to worry. How was he going to get from the airport to a hotel? Had he already booked one? What was the emergency? Did anyone else know he was coming? *Audrey.* She would know. She knew almost everything. She called Audrey. Indeed, she knew. Teddy had arranged to meet the board and shareholders and was heading to Accra to do so. All his travel arrangements had already been finalized by his office in the US and he would be picked up by the hotel shuttle. His meeting with the board was in two days. Bose was not going to be part of the meeting but she will be informed if there was a need for a management meeting after the meeting with the board.

Well, that was helpful. So, when was she going to be told if Teddy had not emailed her? It was getting weird how information was kept under wraps and she was getting uneasy. She decided not to give it much thought. She will focus on what was important and at this point, it was doing her job and achieving her goals. In less than twenty-four hours, she will know why Teddy was meeting the board and shareholders – twenty-four hours seemed like a long way off but, she could wait.

She was lost in her thoughts when she heard a tap on her door. It was Sophia.

"Hi Bose, do you have a minute?"

"Sure, please come in."

"Thank you."

"You look worried. What is wrong? Did someone else resign?"

Sophia smiled.

"Not yet."

"What do you mean 'not yet'? Is there a waiting list of people who want to resign?"

"Not exactly, but I am getting a vibe that I wanted to discuss with you. The sales team is unhappy and a few of them have told their colleagues in other departments that if Maribel continues as their head of department, they will leave the company."

"Why is that?" Bose quizzed, bewildered at the news that just dropped on her lap. As if she already didn't have enough on her plate, she had this to deal with too?

"I think her handling of the passing of Kwame was a bit insensitive. She tried to brush it aside and the team seems to be rebelling in a subtle, but noticeable way. This week alone, three of them have called in sick. One of them has requested for two weeks of leave to seek medical attention and Yomba, who is usually the bubbliest and engaged, seems quite removed from everything around her. I am concerned that if we do not intervene, a few of them will resign."

Bose had a lot to say but simply looked at Sophia for what seemed like forever. Sophia was not sure if Bose had heard what she had said. There was another knock on the door. It was Herdibert.

"Madam, we have an emergency. I presented a cheque for statutory payments and one of them has been returned. Unfortunately, the Social Security guys do not revert to you when your cheque is returned, they simply send you a demand notice with penalties. I have just received it. We have to pay before…"

Bose was looking at Herdibert now. Her attention had been shifted from Sophia to a more urgent matter.

How does a cheque get returned when a finance team is managing cashflow?

"How come, Herdibert. How come the cheque bounced?"

"Well, two weeks ago, I received a number of cheques from the sales team. We issued the cheque for the pension payments against two of those cheques. Unfortunately, those customer cheques were also returned."

"And how is it that you did not find out until now?"

"I didn't just find out, Bose. I found out when the demand notice arrived two days ago. But I've been trying to figure out a plan to pay them. I have tried and nothing is working. We have up to close of this week to make payment or we will be hurled before a court."

"Hmmm, maybe that's the way to go so you can tell the judge why you don't keep track of bank reconciliation."

"Bose, I take a strong exception to that comment. This is not about me. I have a lot on my plate and even though we are constantly monitoring our cashflow and movement of funds, the banking system, as we have it, does not allow us to follow all cheques as we will want to. The clearing process can take a couple of days." Herdibert retorted, visibly upset.

Bose was upset too. She was not going to hide it this time. She was on her feet.

"Herdibert, so when you come to me at this time, what do you expect me to do? Conjure money from heaven? I rely on you to manage the finances of this company. I do not have a solution to this problem save to tell you to please do your job!"

Sophia looked on in utter shock. She had never seen Bose this upset and no one had spoken to Herdibert in this manner ever.

"My job is not to make money for the company. That is *your* job. I will leave you to think about why you are really here and when you're ready to have a civil discussion with me, I will be in my office," Herdibert bellowed with rage. He turned and began to leave.

"Herdibert and Bose, please calm down. We can resolve this without the outbursts. Let me call Maribel. She may have some payments in the pipeline."

Herdibert stopped and gently perched in one of Bose's chairs.

Bose was fuming now.

Who told him to sit down? He should have left. This nonsense about people doing what they like and not doing their job is just rubbish. I've had it. He cannot walk into my office, tell me about a problem and expect me to solve it as well. What nonsense!

Bose's mind was racing. She could feel her heart pounding.

Sophia called Maribel. In a few minutes, all four of them were in a meeting trying to figure out which payments could be collected over the next two days. They figured out a plan. Just as they were about to leave, Bose made an announcement.

"We will meet here every day at 5:00pm to look at the accounts and discuss payments. I will not be caught unawares like this again on critical payments. Please take note. Erastus will send everyone who is required to be in the meetings an email today. It is a standing daily meeting, so whether or not you get a daily reminder, please be here for that meeting at 5:00pm."

"We close at 5:00pm. Why are you setting a meeting for 5:00pm? I cannot be present; I leave the office at 5:00pm," Herdibert uttered flippantly.

"Then, we will meet at 4:00pm. Does that work for you?" Bose's voice was steely now. She could not believe that he expected to leave the office at 5:00pm every single day.

Who does that? She thought.

"Yes, 4:00pm is fine. Have a good evening." Herdibert turned to leave. Maribel was on her way out as well when Bose's words stopped her in her tracks.

"Maribel, please don't leave. Sophia and I will like to have a word with you."

The next ten minutes were more excruciating than the forty-five minutes that just went buy. Maribel churned out justification after justification. She was in no way going to accept that she had been insensitive. She was not even sure why this conversation was happening.

"Sophia, I know how to lead my teams. I have been in management for over fifteen years. I believe this is not you trying to tell me how to do my job?"

And as the banter went on, Bose was forced to play the role of umpire. At the end of the conversation, Bose knew one thing for sure – she was tired. Tired of the company, tired of the work attitude and physically drained. Teddy was going to be in Ghana in another few hours - a perfect time for her to put in a resignation when she meets him.

****

That night when Bose got home, she was sure of two things. First of all, she was going to watch a movie deep into the night and secondly, she was going to convince Mantse that it was time to move on from her job. It turned out that the second issue was easier than the first. She did not have to convince Mantse. He agreed with her immediately. For the movie, she fell soundly asleep on the sofa no sooner had she started watching it. She had reclined in the sofa with her legs propped on her husband's lap. They both fell asleep: one seated, the other lying down. It had been a long stressful day in the lives of this working couple.

CHAPTER ELEVEN

Yomba was having a hard time coping with Kwame's passing and the most irritating part was Maribel's disposition. She was trying as hard as she could to make it seem like nothing happened, and the whole team was hung up on that. Some of them had mentioned to her they no longer felt like working in the company. It was not worth it — "If someone as important as Kwame could be forgotten so quickly, then it means we should not die for this company," Akosua had said.

Yomba did not realize how much anger and grief she was keeping pent up until she *exploded* in a tirade of tears on a busy road on her way to work one fine morning. She was driving unusually fast. A driver appeared out of nowhere and cut in front of her. She slammed hard on her brakes and lunged forward. The other driver drove away. Her knees felt weak and her heart was pounding. She parked for about fifteen minutes, just enough time for her to regain her composure before she continued with her drive.

A few minutes after the near-incident, she was stopped by a traffic policeman. Apparently, she had driven past a red light. She had been totally absent-minded and had not noticed the traffic lights had changed from green to amber and then to red as she sped across. The police officer on a motorcycle followed her for about two minutes and signalled her to stop. The conversation was calm and respectful as the officer pointed out to her what she had done. Yomba was unusually calm with the officer and apologized. There was something in her voice that made the officer realize the young lady was probably in some kind of trouble.

"Madam, you seem very absent-minded. I signalled you for a while before you noticed me. Are you okay?"

Before Yomba could process the import of the question, her lips started to quiver and she started crying. The officer was confused. He was not sure what he had done to cause the young lady to burst into tears. He apologized to her and told her to drive safely. Yomba, sniffed, thanked him and then, drove off slowly. But that was to be a short drive. After less than a minute, she could no longer hold back her tears. She could not see through her tears either so, she parked again and let it all out. Thankfully, everyone was too busy trying to get to work that no one noticed her nor stopped to interact with her. She just let it all out.

What if she had been crashed to death by that recalcitrant driver who dangerously cut in front of her? She would be dead just like Kwame was dead. Just that hers would have been instant and lonelier.

What if she did not die and she had been maimed? What if she was not wearing her seat belt? Would she have been jettisoned out of the car like it was demonstrated in those scary wear-your-seat-belt videos? But the biggest question on her mind was *what will Maribel say?*

"Oh, Yomba is dead. Let's get on with our work."

Was the rushing to work even worth it? Was her work worth all of the stress and insomnia she was developing? Was it worth her life?

After crying for a while, she picked up her phone and sent Maribel a text message.

Hello Maribel, sorry I'm running late today. I am unwell. I will take the day off and get checked. I will let you know if I am well enough to come to work tomorrow. Thank you. The moment she got notification that the message had been sent, she switched off her phone. Today work will wait. She was going to take a break to get *well*. She was not *well*. Her soul was not *well*. She navigated her way in the opposite direction and went home.

****

When Yomba returned from her self-imposed sick leave, she had a query letter waiting for her to respond to. Maribel did not respond to the text message she sent and had rather tried to call her. Yomba's phone was off for most part of the first day and she did not respond to any of Maribel's phone calls on the second day. Maribel was livid. She wrote her a query and told Sophia to ensure that that was the first thing she received "If she ever returned to this office". Yomba returned to work on the third day. When she arrived, she had a note on her desk that read,

"Hello Yomba, please pass by my office as soon as you see this. Thanks, Sophia."

She put her bag down after saying hello to her colleagues and headed to Sophia's office. She could see Maribel sitting in her office as she headed across the hallway to Sophia's.

"Good morning Sophia."

"Hey Yomba! You're back. Good morning."

"Yes please, I'm back."

"I hope you're better. Please, sit down."

"I'm very well, thanks," she responded whilst dropping her weight on the chair Sophia had pointed at.

"So, what did the doctor say and I hope you brought your sick note along today?"

"I did not go to the hospital. I was at home."

"So, you were not really sick." Sophia said it as a statement of fact rather than a question.

"I was unwell, but I didn't go to the hospital," Yomba

responded.

"Well, then I'll have to deduct the two days from your leave days. Also, Maribel asked that you be issued a query letter." Sophia handed it to her.

"You can read it and then come back and let's discuss what your response will be," she added.

"I already know what my response will be, please."

"Tell me."

"I needed a break to prevent a mental breakdown. I needed to rest. I don't mind that you will take this out of my leave days."

"That's fine Yomba, but you were absent from work for two days without permission. That is a disciplinary issue."

"I told my manager I was unwell. I asked for permission."

"No, you informed her – there's a difference."

Yomba was silent for a while.

"Yomba, do you want to tell me what is going on with you?"

"Not really. I am fine. I will take a few hours to consider my response and I will get back to you."

"When you're ready, I'll be available but please get back to me today."

"Yes please."

Yomba headed back to her office. She knew what her response will be. She just did not know how to write it in polite 'corporate-language' without making it sound like she was unperturbed.

Just as she was settling into her seat, her phone rang. It was Abrema, her 'aunty-cousin'.

"Hey Yombs, how are you?"

"I'm doing well o... you saw me this morning so why are you asking me how I am?"

Abrema was laughing gently.

"Because when you were leaving, you were not okay. You didn't look like you wanted to go to work so I just thought I'll check up on you."

"Aww, thank you! I'm well, generally. Just that I have a query to respond to. As much as I try, I do not know how to respond without sounding brash and incredulous."

She dropped her voice to almost a whisper.

"I don't want to tell Maribel my mind. She tried to call me when I was at home and I didn't pick. She is upset."

"Well, it was wrong for you to bolt from work the way you did, Yombs. So, you should apologize to her and explain your actions."

"Apologize? Why?" Yomba exclaimed. She had said it so loudly that her colleagues turned to look in her direction.

"Listen, she's your boss. You didn't do well by vanishing so, do the right thing and apologize," Abrema said, trying to reason with her. She spent the next three minutes explaining her advice to Yomba and still, Yomba was adamant.

"Yombs, you have to choose your battles wisely and fighting your immediate boss won't help you succeed in any way. You won't lose anything by saying sorry. But you can lose your relationship with her by being headstrong."

"I don't want a relationship with her; she is cold and uncaring. All she thinks about is the revenue and her reports. Do you know that she had not once asked me anything about myself? She doesn't know where I live or how I live?"

"But she is not your friend, Yomba. She is your boss. The earlier you realize that and stop asking her to be more than that, the better."

Yomba allowed Abrema to speak for a while and then initiated the end of the conversation.

"We will talk at home. Thank you for checking up on me."

"You're welcome my dear *niece*," Abrema said, stressing on the word 'niece'. She only called her that when she wanted to remind her that she was older and wiser.

"Whatever," she responded sharply.

Yomba knew that Abrema was right with her analysis; she agreed to a large extent with all she said yet, she was not willing to admit it. Holding a grudge with Maribel for some reason seamed like she was honoring the memory of her friend, Kwame and accepting to apologise was equal to losing against keeping her friend's memory alive.

****

Chidi had been looking forward to this trip to Accra for a while. It was not just for the fact that he was going to spend time with his Ghanaian family, but also that he was going to have a break from the hustle and bustle of Lagos. Accra seemed to always be on holiday, compared to Lagos. There was traffic and not *go slow* as they called it in Lagos. The drivers did not constantly have to honk and he appreciated the fact there was less throwing of invectives at each other by road users.

"See dundee united[39]! You just dey form[40] as if you sabi drive. Ode![41]" Another driver had screamed at Chidi one morning on his way to work.

Being called "Ode" early in the morning set his day off on a wrong note. But he was in Accra now. He definitely did not miss the road rage that he had to manage most days commuting to work, in Lagos.

Chidi arrived in Accra on a Friday evening flight. He had asked to be allowed to leave the office at 12noon, dashed to the airport and got on a 5pm flight out of Lagos. The forty-five-minute flight seemed like a 6-hour flight to London. Yomba had offered to pick him up before he could ask her.

That must be a good sign, he thought. *She probably misses me as much as I miss her.*

When he arrived in Accra, it took him about fifty minutes to get through immigration and get his luggage. He could have travelled without a checked bag but his sister, Nene, had insisted he picked up a bag of *stuff* from their mother. She had simply told her mother, "Mama, everything that can fit into a medium-sized Ghana-must-go bag, Chidi will bring it to me. All those spices that I have to search for

---

[39] Nigerian street slang that means "a stupid person"

[40] "Form" here is Nigerian slang that means "to pretend"

[41] Ode – is a Yoruba word meaning "stupid" Pronounced as Ode

here, biko[42], buy them for me." Chidi was unaware of his 'cargo' arrangements until he got a call from his mother two days to his departure.

"Chidi, you have to come by my place to pick up some items for Nene. Please come tomorrow after work, you hear?"

Chidi had no opportunity to ask questions. His mother had the habit of ending calls abruptly. She did not want to "waste call credit on people who can call and visit me", she had once explained. She would, in most instances, flash[43] Chidi and expect him to call her back. There was that one time she had attempted to 'flash' him but Chidi had picked the phone almost immediately it rang because he was texting at the time the call came through.

"Chidi, I am flashing you so call me back now now."

Chidi had burst into laughter but he called her back almost immediately.

"Chidi, why did you pick the call? I was flashing. Now you have caused me to lose credit. You will have to buy my credit for me. Do you understand?"

---

[42]Biko – means please in Ibo

[43] A term that means – a quick call that is not intended for the person recipient to pick. It is usually done to indicate the desire to connect with the other person and solicit a phone call from them.

Her quick phone calls paled into oblivion in comparison to her lengthy face-to-face conversations. Mama Chidi was a quintessential chatterbox.

Chidi had arrived in his parents' home on Thursday evening after work. He was happy to make the stop because it meant he could wait out the traffic for a while. What he had not prepared for was the bag of 'stock fish, cray fish and a collection of spices' that would easily qualify him to pass as a chef of a *buka*[44] on his way to a cooking competition. He had taken a look at the bag and its contents and said to his mother:

"Mama, no o, there is no way I am travelling with this bag. The whole airport will just start smelling and before you know it, I am the cynosure of the airport."

"Cyno-what? Look here young man, your sister has been in Ghana for a while now and misses home. She wants to cook with original Ibo spices and you will take them to her."

He smiled at his mother. She was speaking to him as if he was that ten-year-old son who had to be compelled to go to Sunday mass.

"Mama, I am going to visit Nene, but the main reason I am going to Accra is to see Yomba. See your son – such a fine young man like me; do you want me to meet a young

[44] A Hausa word that means – "side of the road" but has come to represent street food joints.

lady I like with a bag of food? I would even be smelling of fish." As he spoke, he put his arm around his mother's shoulders, hoping to convince her into changing her mind.

His mother looked up, stared at him, smiled and said:

"Chidi, she would like you more because she will think you know how to cook."

That was it! He did not argue any further. He even, surprisingly, liked the sound of that. It settled the matter. It will definitely be nice if Yomba thought that he could not only cook, but can actually pick the right spices to make his food taste yummy.

He was approaching the exit of the terminal and could see Yomba smiling broadly at him. As he approached her, he noticed, to his surprise, his nieces: Gracie and Gloria in tow.

"Uncle Chidi!" They ran into his arms.

This was a pleasant surprise. Could it mean that Nene was also at the airport?

He was now standing face to face with Yomba. She spontaneously hugged him. Even before he could reach out, she was already holding unto his neck with her two arms and hugging him tight. It felt like the best thing in the world but it ended too quickly – Gracie and Gloria wanted to be carried and at that moment, he wished they were not there.

"Where did they come from?" he asked.

Yomba was laughing. She had achieved the objective for bringing them along.

"I wanted to surprise you so I convinced Nene to allow me to bring them. She was not sure I could handle them but she agreed. They have been okay so far. Apart from the wanting to go to the washroom ever so often, we've managed well. And you're here! So, I'm happy," Yomba responded. Her eyes glistening under the bright lights at the airport.

They proceeded to leave the airport after struggling to get the girls strapped in because they were so excited about the airport and did not want to settle down. They finally did and Yomba headed in the direction of Nene's home. They drove for the first few minutes interacting with the girls who had questions for their uncle but, it was not long before they went quiet. Gloria fell asleep first, and then Gracie.

"They must be tired."

"Oh, they are. They spent about 30 minutes just running around the terminal and giggling. At a point, I was scared they will fall down and hurt themselves because of the tiled floors but they didn't. They are so energetic!"

Chidi smiled. He liked the fact that Yomba was comfortable around his nieces. He assumed she had not noticed his bag of fish. They drove the rest of the way heartily chatting. Yomba will drop him off and then pick him up as early as she could the next morning for a long line up of activities. He was in Accra for five days and they had to make the best out of those days.

****

Bose's resignation was unexpected. She had a meeting with Teddy the evening of his arrival and the next day, she submitted her resignation to the board chair and then informed Sophia by a phone call. Her decision had coincided with Altimatum's decision to release their shareholding in DataMine. Teddy had come into town to communicate the decision to the board and shareholders before an official communication would be issued from their Headquarters. They were no longer interested in the business and had decided to sell their shares. The board expressed their surprise but indicated that they will accept the decision and cooperate with Altimatum throughout the process of their exit. As a majority shareholder, Altimatum was going to ensure that their exit and sale of shares brought about minimum impact on their global business and reputation.

"Our greatest concern is that the staff members and customers will have no sense of insecurity throughout this process and we request that that remains of paramount concern to all of us. Additionally, our communication to the public will not include any indications of our dissatisfaction with how our relationship has been handled over these last eighteen months so you can be assured of our strictest confidentiality on that score," Teddy had said.

Altimatum's decision to withdraw from the partnership with DataMine was made swiftly and without much debate at the Global Headquarters. The year was winding down and the business had started to evaluate its global operation. The West African expansion plan was ambitious but it was not turning to be half of what they expected. They decided it was best to opt out of it and spend a bit more time in their domestic operations, using a different approach – engaging franchisees.

Teddy's trip to Accra was supposed to achieve two main things: to have a meeting with the board and shareholders of DataMine and secondly, to offer Bose the opportunity to roll out the new strategy.

Bose said no.

"Thanks for the offer Teddy. I appreciate your vote of confidence but, I will not be able to take up this appointment."

"Do you not want to spend some time thinking about it? Maybe a few weeks? It will take us at least eight weeks to wind down here and then maybe another few weeks for us to set up the needed meetings to begin to engage you. So really, this will really be starting in about 3 months."

"Thanks Teddy. But, no thanks. I can have this conversation with you again in three months, but right now, I do not want you to have the impression I am interested in it. In fact, I want to think about what I want to do generally and that is not just about DataMine."

"Bose, that's fine. We will speak to you again in three months."

"Thanks Teddy."

"No problem."

They spent the rest of the time together talking about a range of issues – the threat of impeachment of Donald Trump, the rising threat of nuclear war due to the activities of North Korea and Iran and even the always-prevalent issue of *jollof wars* – who made the best jollof in West Africa? At the end of their meeting, Bose was happy she had made time to meet Teddy. He was meeting the DataMine board the following morning, but had decided to meet her first. The timing was perfect for her. She would resign immediately and work with all stakeholders to successfully execute Altimatum's exit. It would seem like a natural exit for her – the outside world will never know that she had already decided to resign. They will simply assume that she left with the 'foreign' company.

Bose submitted her resignation to Audrey just before the board meeting with Teddy." Audrey had looked at her quizzingly.

"I've decided to leave, Audrey."

"I suspected it will come to this Bose. Even though I am sad to see you go, I understand your decision. I will hand it over to the Board Chair after this meeting."

"Thank you, Audrey."

"You're welcome."

After the surprise announcement by Teddy, Mr. Sinare was handed Bose's resignation.

"I spoke to her, sir. She had made up her mind," Audrey said to him as if in response to an unasked question."

"Spoke to who?" Carl asked.

"Bose has resigned," Audrey said with a hint of sarcasm.

"Oh wow," Carl exclaimed. He had been on his way out of the meeting room when he overheard the conversation between Audrey and Mr. Sinare, and joined, uninvited.

"Well, with Altimatum leaving, I believe it is the right time for her to also leave. We will appoint a new Country Manager when they exit finally. Please write to her and accept her resignation. I hope she has indicated her notice period and is prepared to properly serve it."

Audrey handed him the letter to read.

He looked surprised but masked it with a bit of bravado.

No one had resigned in his company, willingly. He always compelled them to or fired them outrightly. Bose had broken the jinx. He did not see this coming. He was upset.

"Well, good riddance… we will find someone else," he said whilst handing the letter back to Audrey.

Mr. Sinare, Teddy, Bose and Audrey later had a meeting to map out a plan for the exit of Altimatum. Maribel will shadow Bose in the transition period until a substantive Country Manager was appointed. Altimatum had agreed to sell back their majority shares to DataMine and receive payment over twenty-four months. That was a very generous offer and Carl could not hide his excitement. The arrangement essentially meant he had enough capital to continue running the business whilst looking for a new investor.

****

Mantse had settled into a routine at the University and Bose was winding down with her job at DataMine. He was happy with the version of his wife he was seeing recently. She came home much earlier each day and did not just flop into the sofa looking spent. Initially, he felt her complaints about work were just her inability to adjust to the culture of the organisation and possibly being away from familiar surroundings. But, he soon enough realized that it was not just Bose. He worried about her not having a job and being idle. For as long as he had known her, she was always working

– active, busy and working. Maybe it was a good time for her to slow down then. They had decided that she will wait for at least three months before she made a decision on her next move. She was already talking about starting her consultancy in Accra. For now, he preferred not to think about another 'ride', the DataMine rollercoaster had been fast enough. Now, he was going to focus on his family and getting his Bose back to her full bubbly self.

****

Chidi had come to Ghana for one main reason – he was considering a move to Ghana. The bank had advertised an opening that was going to be filled by an internal candidate. It would be a promotion for him and he would have to move to Ghana to be the head of a new unit being set. The only snag was his office was going to be in Takoradi – the Oil City.

Ghana had discovered crude oil in commercial quantities in 2007 and that had attracted a new wave of investment and business opportunities. His bank had set up a business unit to support the oil exploration companies and wanted it located in Takoradi. He was being offered the opportunity to lead one of the units for the new operation. When he was told the new role will take him to Ghana, he was excited for two reasons – he was going as an expatriate and because he would be close to Nene, her family, and of course, Yomba. He wanted to go to Takoradi and see how it was like before finally accepting the offer to move. Yomba had agreed to fly in with him on a return trip. Thankfully, there were domestic flights that could take them in first thing in the morning and return at the end of the day.

They arrived at the domestic terminal of the Kotoka International Airport in time for their early morning flight. It was a Saturday and Yomba had picked him up at 5:30am, in time to get to the airport, check-in and leave on a 7:00am flight. At the airport, Chidi experienced a side of Ghana he had never encountered. They had just parked and were heading to the terminal when a young man standing in front of the terminal offered to sell them padlocks. Chidi found it surprising that anyone will try to sell padlocks to them since they were not carrying any luggage.

"Ah ah no now, we don't even have luggage," he said and smiled.

"You can buy for your wife, maybe next time she can use it," the young man responded

"No, thank you," Chidi responded as he continued on his way, Yomba now slightly ahead of him. He was also a few steps away from the vendor.

"Or she is not your wife? Are you stealing her away from us? You Nigerians come here and take all our beautiful women and then our businesses too. We know you."

Chidi was dumbfounded. Yomba stopped and looked at the vendor with a stoic look that could tell him she was in no way going to tolerate his insulting behaviour.

"Oh Ohemaa,[45] make you no bore o.[46]"

Chidi was not sure how to react so he took a cue from Yomba and continued walking. After they had checked in and were seated waiting for boarding, Chidi could no longer hold his curiosity.

"Not that I don't like the fact that he assumed you're my wife o, but what was that about? Are Nigerians not welcome here? The guy sounded very offensive and hostile."

"Pay him no attention, Chidi. He was just being funny."

"That was not funny."

"You're right. It was not funny. It was hostile. We've had some anti-foreign sentiments lately, especially among the traders. There were, recently, altercations with foreigners who own shops in some of the business districts – the locals forcing them to close their shops and citing a Ghanaian law that prohibits foreigners from engaging in retail business. Even though they have the law on their side, there have been some excesses."

---

[45] Twi word for "Princess"

[46] Pidgin – loosely translated as "Oh Princess, don't be angry"

"Sounds scary, especially with what has happened in South Africa recently. Several Nigerians had to flee violent attacks in cities like Gauteng and Durban."

"Hmm, I followed that. Fortunately, there are long historical ties between Ghana and Nigeria, including that time we spelt Nigeria with goals."

"Eh, what are you talking about?"

"Well, my dear friend, in 1955, the Black Stars scored the Super Eagles seven - nil. How many letters are there in the word Nigeria – seven – so we spelt Nigeria," Yomba said teasingly.

Chidi was laughing. He was aware of the football rivalry between Ghana and Nigeria but he had never paid much attention to the history of it. He did not challenge Yomba's assertion because he had no basis to.

Their flight into Takoradi was on time and they spent about three hours driving around the city. They drove first of all to the Market Circle – what was considered the hub of brisk business in that city. They had lunch and then headed back to the airport. Chidi wanted to move to Ghana, but a four-hour drive from Accra seemed too far for him. He will make the decision later. He liked the serenity of Ghana but the incident at the airport left a sour taste in his mouth.

CHAPTER TWELVE

A few months passed and Bose and Altimatum Inc had finally parted ways with DataMine Ltd. Her last few days were not without incident. Maribel was appointed Acting Country Manager, Sophia put in a resignation and Herdibert had been unwell and admitted in hospital the last two weeks before she left. His hospitalization had given everyone a scare.

He was sitting in a meeting with his team – working on a priority list for payments that were due to vendors. All of a sudden, he slumped slightly in his chair. Initially, everyone thought he was asleep – but it was so unusual for him to fall asleep during a meeting. One of his colleagues tried to wake him up and he very faintly responded. That was what triggered their anxiety. Herdibert was almost unconscious. They quickly rushed him to a nearby clinic only to learn that he had experienced a transient ischemic attack.

"A trans-kini?[47]" Bose had asked when the doctor told her.

[47]Kini in Yoruba means "what" – trans-what?

"That's a mini-stroke, Madam. He is quite lucky. He just needs to pay more attention to his blood pressure going forward. At his age, the risk factors are quite glaring and we will like to monitor him for a while before discharging him."

'For a while' ended up being two weeks. Herdibert had been diagnosed with borderline high blood pressure two years prior and was advised to make some lifestyle changes.

"You want me to stop eating all these things!" He had exclaimed to the dietician at the clinic who was trying as hard as he could to explain portion sizes and food items to avoid.

Herdibert was not having any of it. He left the dietician's office and went straight back into his regular lifestyle.

Bose visited him in the hospital on her last working day. He was in good spirits.

"I think this two-week break was very good for me. Interestingly, even though I've been away from the office, nothing has gone wrong. All the payments we had to make have been made and life is going on. No one died," he joked.

"Indeed! I think, sometimes, we worry too much and, in the end, we physically harm ourselves. That's why I am not going to do anything until the end of the year. I'll just chill."

"I hope you can stay without doing anything, Madam. I've seen how hard you work," Herdibert said and Bose knew that that was the best compliment he has ever given her.

"I will try," she replied smilingly.

Herdibert smiled at her knowingly. With the benefit of hindsight, he wished he had taken more deliberate breaks. His health may have been better.

"Thank you very much for everything Herdibert. I hope you get discharged soon."

"Thank you too, for coming. It's been good working with you."

"That is mutual Mr. Sosu" Bose said as they shook hands before parting ways.

When she had arrived at DataMine almost three years ago, Herdibert was one individual she felt she will not be able to get along with. He seemed laid back and bureaucratic and she wanted everything to be done 'now'. They had a few run-ins but, eventually, had learnt how to get along and become cordial work colleagues.

****

Chidi turned down the offer of a promotion and move to Ghana. He had discussed his plans with a mentor of his and even though it was difficult, he decided to stay in Lagos.

It was a tough call because he was looking forward to being closer to Yomba.

"I believe the government over-hyped the impact of this oil find on the local economy and has created a false sense of hope among the people. Within a few months of the oil discovery, the cost of living in Takoradi skyrocketed! But guess what, after a few years, they've realized there has to be a more deliberate effort to harness the opportunities to benefit the locals. What your bank wants to do is a novelty, but I don't expect that it will survive after two years. If it doesn't survive, you will have to return to Lagos, but as what? That move back will create an issue for you professionally."

Chidi had to think with his head instead of his heart. He loved the serenity of Ghana but, he realized he would be making a professionally risky move if he accepted the promotion. He had seen a similar scenario play out with a colleague who was transferred to Sierra Leone to start a branch. She was more senior in the organisation and unfortunately, when there was an Ebola outbreak in that country, she was recalled. She had been designated the title of 'Country Business Development Lead' which was equivalent to the role of a Regional Branch supervisor in their Nigerian operation. When she returned, there was no vacancy at that level in the organisation and she eventually resigned.

"I'll still visit Accra as often as I can, Yomba. And if you agree to marry me, maybe I will move and come live with you."

Yomba laughed at Chidi's attempt to make light of his decision.

"Marry you? But you've not asked me to marry you for me to decline?"

"So, are you saying yes?"

"You've not asked. And if you have to ask, you have to ask me well. Haven't you seen those nice men who go down on one knee and propose?"

Chidi laughed out loudly.

"Those guys are not serious in life. Do they realize that after proposing in public they still have to go and see the lady's parents and in Africa, the parents can say no?"

"You sound just like an Uncle of mine. He has vowed that if any of his five daughters come home with a man who had already proposed to her with a ring, he will refuse to give out his daughter to such a man. "A man who is serious about my daughter must come to me first," he had said." They both laughed.

This was the third time Chidi was joking about the subject of marriage and Yomba played along. She was not going to make it into a big deal – the timing for her was wrong. She was focusing on surviving at her job and she did not want to complicate matters by getting married to Chidi and having to figure out where they will live – Lagos or Accra.

****

After consistently promising to visit her friend, Adaora finally made it to Accra at Christmas. She reluctantly agreed to spend the week with Bose and Mantse in their apartment.

"Biko,[48] I need to be able to sleep well in the night. I don't want to hear your children crying and you shouting at them," she had joked.

"My children are no longer babies. When was the last time you even saw them? It will be a good opportunity for them to bond with their Aunty Adaora and you can use the money you would have used to pay for the hotel to buy me a bottle of Coco Chanel."

"So na perfume you want wey you dey want make I no book hotel for Accra?[49] I go buy for you. That's not a problem at all. You know cash mama dey town[50]."

---

[48]Please in Ibo

[49] Pidgin: Is it because you want perfume, I should not book a hotel?

[50] Pidgin: Mama Cash is in town

"No now, I want you close. I don't want to drive to see you. That's all."

Adaora agreed. She had planned to see a few sites outside Accra but generally, her trip was to spend time with Bose and help her figure out her next move.

****

Mantse had been appointed as Dean of Students at the university where he taught. During one of their University Council meetings, he had his first taste of what it meant not to fit in. The Vice Chancellor had asked for a volunteer from the council to meet with the Student Representative Council about an issue they had reported related to the use of their dining halls for events hosted by non-university members. Since the issue related to students, Mantse quickly volunteered.

"I will be happy to meet them to discuss this. I have quite a good relationship with the SRC executive."

"That you have a good relationship with the SRC executive is the main reason why you should not be the one meeting them. Those kids do not respect their elders; they need to meet someone who is firm and resilient and definitely not a young man like you," retorted the Head of the College of Sciences, failing to hide his dislike for Mantse.

"Okay, I will leave the decision on who will be on the committee to the Dean of Students to decide," the Vice Chancellor had said, in an attempt to end any possible banter.

Mantse, a forty-five-year-old man was being referred to as a 'young man like you'. He chuckled a little and then responded.

"I know how they think, even though I am several years older than them, it helps to be able to relate with them properly so we can better understand what their issues are."

"I agree with you, Dean. Please go ahead and report to us at the next meeting."

The air had gone tense. As no one expected the Vice Chancellor to give his support to the 'young man'.

Theirs was a meeting of *elders* and to be an elder, you had to be in your late fifties and approaching retirement age. Of a council of fifteen members, there was only one woman and one 'young man'. After Mantse was first nominated as Dean of Students, he had attended his first council meeting. As was his habit, he arrived at the venue five minutes to time and happened to be the only one seated when one of the council members walked in.

"Young man, there is a council meeting going to be held here. Are you lost?"

Mantse rose, extended his hand and introduced himself.

"I am Mantse, I am the new Dean of Students."

"Oh, I see. You would easily have passed for one of our students or, at best, a teaching assistant. I am Professor Sawyer," the council member said as they shook hands.

"Let's blame that on genes," Mantse replied and both laughed heartily and proceeded to have a conversation whilst they waited for everyone else to arrive.

As they walked in, several of them glanced in the direction of Professor Sawyer and Mantse. Professor Sawyer knowingly introduced Mantse to as many as quizzed with their eyes and before the meeting could commence, they all knew the *young man*.

"Talk about a gerontocracy!" he said to Bose later that evening as they discussed it.

"So, my almost greying old man is a young man to some people," Bose could not hide her amusement.

"You are going to have an interesting journey there."

"I can bet on it. It was a bit different at the Unilag, but since I was not a council member, it was not that glaring. Now, I'm on the University Council with *elders*."

"Maybe you should not show up for your next meeting in khaki trousers and a short sleeve shirt."

"Ah! So, you want me to wear a three-piece suit just to show that I am old? Then I might as well go and find one of my father's Irish tweed jackets and match it with a pair of corduroy trousers. I can even find me a pair of crepe-soled shoes, which are still in vogue. I'll fit right into the mould of the 'village headmaster'."

Bose was laughing so hard there were tears were in her eyes.

"It is thirty degrees Celsius and upwards each day in this city of ours. I will not kill myself."

"You'll be fine. I'm sure of it," Bose assured him with an understanding smile.

After a semester, Mantse continued to have his small incidents with other members of the university community but that did not deter him from settling in nicely.

Bose was working from home now – assisting Adaora and her family set up partnerships with Ghanaian businesses for a new product they were going to import from China. She, occasionally, had to meet prospective partners in town, but mainly in a hotel for a few minutes and then she was back home. The children had settled well in school and were happy to spend some weekends with Mantse's mother who they called *Aunty Naa*, not of their own volition, but because she had specifically forbidden them from calling her "grandma".

****

Yomba continued working at DataMine and after some months of working in an acting capacity of sales manager, she was confirmed to that position due to her diligence and resourcefulness. She was excited, but also sceptical. Now that she was the Sales Manager, she was going to report to Maribel directly. The thought of it was scary. Her Bosephobia had gradually eased away as she got a better grip on how to present her reports in a way that projected progress and consistency and of course, once Bose stopped attending their sales meetings, the phobia changed its name. The fear of Maribel, however, was not a fear that kept her up at night, it was the one that made sure she did not cross paths with her at work or have any query-related run-ins. The new human resources manager was pleasant and relatable but had told her that she would be dismissed if she had two more queries. Yomba decided to steer clear of trouble and so far, so good.

****

It was the end of another year, there were parties everywhere – companies were having their end of year parties and friends were hosting other friends. Bose and Mantse were invited by a Nigerian couple they had met, to join them for a Boxing Day party. Bose was excited that she would possibly meet other Nigerian professionals and make some new friends. But she was more excited to get away from their two champions for an evening. She was looking forward to the music and the dancing.

When they arrived, Bose quickly realized she was going to have a really good time. The DJ was blasting music from Sir Shina Peters, who had been one of her favourite musicians growing up in Lagos. He was an icon of the genre known as *juju music*. She started to dance as they approached their hosts.

"Hello Nene and Emeka! Thank you very much for inviting us."

"You're welcome Bose. Doc, how now?[51]" Nene, Bose, Emeka and Mantse exchanged pleasantries.

In the middle of their conversation, Bose noticed a young lady who was smiling broadly whilst approaching her, hand in hand with a dashing young man. The young lady looked familiar.

"Hello Madam Bose. It's Yomba."

"Oooh wow! Yomba. It's so nice to see you again. It's been a while. How is DataMine? How is everyone?"

"We are all very well, thanks. I am now the Sales Manager so there's a bit more work to be done."

---

[51] How are you? "Now" does not have much significance in this phrase.

"Congratulations. I always knew you'd be a star."

"Thank you, madam,"

"Oh, so you already know Yomba,' Nene said, joining in the conversation.

"Then, let me introduce you to Chidi, my younger brother. He is Yomba's friend," she said the word friend in a drawn-out manner, almost not sure if the word was appropriate.

"Nice to finally meet you Madam Bose. I have heard so much about you."

"I hope there were good things o?" she asked, not sure if Yomba had any good words for her.

"Errmm ..." Chidi was holding back his laughter, but everyone else was already laughing.

"I'm sure Yomba had some things to say about me. We worked together at a very difficult time for DataMine. Thank God it's better now."

"That's true, but it's not really better. I have just figured out how to work around the system," Yomba replied proudly.

"Well, this is a party and we did not come here to discuss *wok*," Nene interrupted.

"Everyone, enjoy your evening. There's enough food and drinks and of course, good music. Yomba, don't worry. I've asked the DJ to play some Shatta Wale and Stonebwoy for you at some point. But you have to dance o," Nene quipped, teasing the young generation with their choice of music.

"No problem! As long as Chidi will dance with me," she replied, indirectly poking fun at Chidi, the man with two left feet.

Nene and Emeka began to laugh. Chidi was an awful dancer and he avoided dancing as a person will avoid catching a plague. Chidi knew why they were laughing.

"Today, I will shame my enemies," he said and pulled Yomba away.

The evening proceeded nicely. Bose, Mantse, Yomba, Chidi, Nene and Emeka, all in the same place. Yomba looked around the party.

Who would have thought I would be in the same party as Madam Bose, dancing to Nigerian music with a stranger I met on a plane?

Life is interesting and the world is small.

****

Yomba stayed at the party until late. Chidi was staying with Nene, as usual, and so was really not going to *go* anywhere. Yomba had planned to leave by 10pm. It was 11:30pm and as it stood now, she was not sure of when she wanted to leave or *if* she would leave that is. She was sitting at a table with Chidi and three other guests she had met at the party. The conversations were engaging, and she was having a good time.

"Oh wow! It's almost midnight. I need to leave," she said.

"Well, you don't have to leave. You can stay. I'm sure the twins will be very happy to see you in the morning," Chidi replied.

Yomba laughed at the prospect.

"So, where will I sleep?"

"With the twins. There's enough space for you on the floor."

They both began to laugh.

"No, thank you. I will head off now."

"Maybe we should get married so that we can actually sleep in the same room."

"Errm, is that your proposal?"

"Maybe. Let's go. You can say goodbye to Nene and Emeka."

They proceeded hand in hand to where Nene and Emeka were.

"Thank you very much for inviting me. I had a good evening," Yomba said, hugging Nene.

"You're welcome my dear. Chidi is always so happy when you're around. I am beginning to think that one day he will not go back to Lagos."

"I asked her to marry me so we can stay together. She laughed at me."

"Ah ah… did you ask her nicely?"

"No o, please don't mind him. He did not ask me," Yomba responded shyly.

"Nawa for you[52]. Do you want me to kneel down and ask you to marry me?"

Yomba was laughing loudly.

"Maybe…" she replied dragging her words.

Yomba said her final goodbyes and Chidi walked with her to her car.

---

[52]Pidgin: Wow or you have just blown me away

"I hope you enjoyed yourself, Yomba."

"Yes, I did. It's been long time since I had so much fun. Please tell Nene to have another party over the Easter weekend so I can come and eat free food, dance and listen to good music."

"I thought you were going to add 'so I can spend time with you'."

"Oh yes, that too."

She leaned forward to hug him and pulled back as quickly as the hug started.

"I will ask you to marry me when I am ready to marry Chidi."

"I see! Well, I hope you will be ready soon o. Because I have been ready since I met you."

"Says the man who doesn't want to kneel," Yomba teased.

She moved to sit in her car.

"Good night Chidi."

"Good night my future wife."

THE END